THE STAFFORDSHIRE BULL TERRIER

Cynthia P. Gallagher

The Staffordshire Bull Terrier

Project Team
Editor: Stephanie Fornino
Copy Editor: Joann Woy
Indexer: Elizabeth Walker
Design: Patricia Escabi
Series Design: Stephanie Krautheim and Mada Design
Series Originator: Dominique De Vito

T.F.H. Publications
President/CEO: Glen S. Axelrod
Executive Vice President: Mark E. Johnson
Publisher: Christopher T. Reggio
Production Manager: Kathy Bontz

T.F.H. Publications, Inc.
One TFH Plaza
Third and Union Avenues
Neptune City, NJ 07753

Printed and bound in China
08 09 10 11 12   1 3 5 7 9 8 6 4 2

Library of Congress Cataloging-in-Publication Data
Gallagher, Cynthia P.
  The Staffordshire bull terrier / Cynthia P. Gallagher.
      p. cm.
  Includes index.
  ISBN 978-0-7938-3682-6 (alk. paper)
  1. Staffordshire bull terrier. I. Title.
SF429.S85G35 2008
636.755'9—dc22
                              2007052140

This book has been published with the intent to provide accurate and authoritative information in regard to the subject matter within. While every reasonable precaution has been taken in preparation of this book, the author and publisher expressly disclaim responsibility for any errors, omissions, or adverse effects arising from the use or application of the information contained herein. The techniques and suggestions are used at the reader's discretion and are not to be considered a substitute for veterinary care. If you suspect a medical problem consult your veterinarian.

The Leader In Responsible Animal Care For Over 50 Years!®
www.tfh.com

TABLE OF CONTENTS

HISTORY
of the Staffordshire Bull Terrier

There's a certain stateliness about all things British, even dog breeds. No one can deny that the Springer Spaniel or the English Setter carries a particular pride in his stride. Now one of the United Kingdom's favorite breeds is finding favor in the United States: the Staffordshire Bull Terrier (also known as the Staffy). Currently one of the top ten most popular breeds in the United Kingdom, the Staffy has steadily gained popularity in the United States, finding his way into the hearts and homes of Americans with an appreciation for his handsome appearance, loving temperament, and easy grooming care.

The Staffy officially belongs to the American Kennel Club's (AKC) Terrier Group but is acknowledged as one of the "bully breeds," a collection of dog breeds whose development hearkens back to the ancient warring and fighting dogs. Other bully breeds include the American Pit Bull Terrier, the American Staffordshire Terrier, the Boxer, and the American Bulldog. Because of their physical resemblance to one another, all too often these related breeds are lumped together under the term "pit bull," an ambiguous name used either in ignorance or uncertainty over an individual dog's actual breed. Because of their historical fighting origins and today's illicit dog fighting practices, the name "pit bull" is associated with viciousness, aggression, and menace to society.

In reality, the Staffy is the very antithesis of a "bully" as we know it. Bully breeds in general and Staffies in

The American Kennel Club (AKC)

The AKC is the oldest dog breed registry in the US, a parent club of breed clubs from all over the country. Its bylaws and constitution were officially adopted on October 22, 1884, in New York City. By the 1920s, the AKC had divided competition show dogs into five groups: Sporting Dogs (which, at the time, included all hounds), Working Dogs, Terriers, Toys, and Non-Sporting breeds. Dogs who captured the Best of Breed (BOB) title from among other dogs of the same breed competed with BOB winners of other breeds within the same Group. The five Group winners went on to compete for the coveted Best in Show (BIS) title.

The purpose of the AKC remains unchanged since its inception: to set standards within each breed to which breeders aspire in their litters. Conformation shows continue to be a platform to determine which dogs are best suited to breed the next generation of champions who most closely epitomize the ideal characteristics of their breed.

particular are known for their deep affection for humans, especially children. In England, the Staffy is often referred to as the "nanny dog" because of his protective and nurturing instincts. The breed's strong sense of loyalty, boundless courage and tenacity, and intelligent, playful personality have long made it the companion dog of choice in England. Happily, America is now discovering the appeal of this wonderful breed.

EARLY DEVELOPMENT OF THE STAFFY

During ancient times of Roman circuses and barbaric warfare, there existed no specific dog breed names as we know them today. Dog types were named for the kind of work they did. The Staffy's origins lie in early Greek Mastiff-type dogs called Molossians who flourished throughout the Roman Empire, providing "entertainment" by fighting all manner of creature, from human to elephant. Impressed by their courage, professional warriors took these prized canine gladiators into battle with them. One Egyptian pharaoh kept 2,000 fighting dogs in his own army.

During the Middle Ages, Mastiffs in battle were supplanted by mechanical weapons and armaments, so the nobility began using animals as guard dogs and hunters of large marauders, such as bears and wolves. Their strength and tenacity were not diminished in their new role, and admiring Europeans began matching them against other beasts in mini-spectacles, and ultimately, in full-fledged "sports." Bull- and bearbaiting became particularly popular using dogs from Germany called *bullenbeisser* and *barenbeisser*, smaller varieties of warring dogs who would fearlessly attack a chained bull or bear and ultimately bring it down. Breeders soon

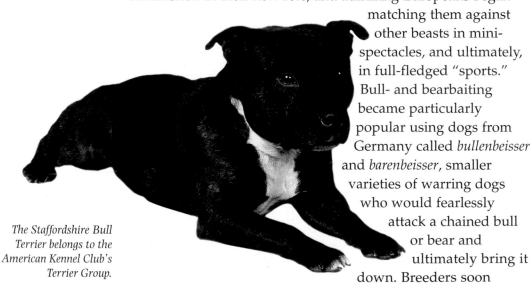

The Staffordshire Bull Terrier belongs to the American Kennel Club's Terrier Group.

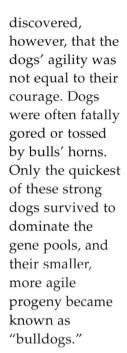

discovered, however, that the dogs' agility was not equal to their courage. Dogs were often fatally gored or tossed by bulls' horns. Only the quickest of these strong dogs survived to dominate the gene pools, and their smaller, more agile progeny became known as "bulldogs."

BREED HISTORY IN ENGLAND

During the sixth century BCE, Phoenician traders made their way to England along with their Mastiff-type Molossian dogs who had fought so ferociously in battles and entertainment spectacles.

The Staffy's Ancestors: Fighting Dogs

In Europe, these warrior dogs were utilized for more than blood sports. They made excellent guard dogs for tradesmen, and their gameness, or willingness, to enter into a conflict and see it to the end, was valued by butchers and farmers who used the "bulldogs" to catch and hold livestock for castration or slaughter. In fact, it was commonly believed that a baited bull yielded more tender and more nutritious meat. Butchers could be penalized for neglecting to bait bulls prior to slaughter.

Unfortunately, the entertainment of watching animals fight one another grew in popularity during the ensuing centuries. Cockfighting, bullbaiting, and dog fighting provided the masses with diversions from the drudgery of daily life. Without music, books, and the other educational pursuits with which the gentry occupied themselves, the working class had to make do with whatever entertainment they could muster. In a perverse irony, the rise of dog fighting helped put food on the table for many an unemployed Briton and became an endeavor taken very seriously by participants.

It became clear that the only way to have a "fair" fight was if the dogs were of equal size. This turned the pastime of dog fighting into a gambling opportunity quite lucrative for the owners of winning dogs. The entertainment grew into a widespread subculture that became a way of life. Wage-earning winning dogs commonly received star treatment in their homes. It was even reported that, to protect the owner's livelihood, the family dog was well fed even if the children went hungry. Official dog fighting rules were established and record books created and maintained.

The Advent of the Bull-and-Terrier

In the quest for a breed of fighting dog that was as agile as it was tenacious, people crossbred the large Bulldog with terriers, smaller dogs developed to follow small game into underground (*terra*) dens. The resulting dog was called the Bull-and-Terrier, or Half-and-Half, a medium-sized dog who was both fierce and nimble in the fighting pit.

The Bull-and-Terrier was as gentle and affectionate with humans as he was aggressive and powerful against his opponents in the ring. This was a necessity, as "professional"

Timeline in England

- 1935: The Staffy breed standard was drafted in England by Joe Dunn and officially adopted at the first meeting of the UK's Staffordshire Bull Terrier Club. Later that year, the breed was recognized by the Kennel Club (KC).
- 1936: The first Staffy, Cross Guns Johnson, owned by Joe Dunn, is entered into the Crufts Dog Show, winning in his class.
- 1937: Staffy popularity expands from the Midlands to southern England, where London-area fanciers started their own regional club. Today, there are 18 breed clubs throughout the UK.
- 1938: The Birmingham National Dog Show awarded the first Challenge Certificates to the new breed of Staffies.
- 1939: A total of 15 Staffies earned entry into the KC Stud Book.
- 1946: The first championship show for Staffies is held by the Southern Counties Staffordshire Bull Terrier Society, attracting 300 dogs.
- 1948: The Staffy breed standard is amended to require a shorter size of dog.

fighting dogs lived with their owners' families. Moreover, fighting dog handlers interacted constantly with the dogs. Before each fight, a handler would wash his opponent's dog to make sure that no poisonous substance had been applied to his skin. Handlers were also required to be in the fighting pit with the dogs, acting as coaches. None of this would have been possible if Bull-and-Terriers were aggressive toward humans. Any demonstrated aggression toward humans was viewed as a serious flaw in an otherwise desirable bloodline. Oddly enough, this mentality corresponds directly with the modern purpose of using the conformation show ring to determine which dogs should be bred. The "survival of the fittest" principle is demonstrated at its worst with pit fighting and at its best with contemporary dog showing.

The AKC and KC's breed standards dictate that the Staffy Bull can weigh no more than 40 pounds (18 kg).

The Humane Acts of 1835

The heinous baiting and fighting activity was finally banned in England by the Humane Acts of 1835, but unfortunately, it continued in secret. It wasn't feasible to stage a clandestine bullbaiting, but it was easy to pit two dogs against each other in a cellar or back room.

The Emergence of the Staffy Bull Terrier

Toward the end of the nineteenth century, breeders of the Bull-and-Terrier branched out into new sub-breeds. One of these groups became a distinctive breed, ultimately acknowledged by Great Britain's Kennel Club (KC) as the Bull Terrier. Selective breeding in this dog produced an elongated head and general appearance quite different from the Bull-and-Terrier, who had become especially popular in the Staffordshire area of England. To avoid confusion with the new Bull Terrier breed, the Half-and-Half (or Bull-and-Terrier) was renamed the Staffordshire Bull Terrier (Staffy or Staffy Bull) in 1935.

The first Staffy breed standard was drafted in 1935 by committed breeder Joe Dunn and adopted at the first meeting of the UK's Staffordshire Bull Terrier Club. The breed was recognized by the KC later that year and allowed to enter dog shows. Oddly enough, the Staffy breed's pioneers were not pleased with the Staffy's entrance into the show world, fearing that his game temperament would be endangered and the true heart of the breed lost. They considered the true Staffy to be a fighting dog and one who should remain so.

In addition to the debate about characteristics, controversy emerged over the Staffy's desired size. The original breed standard called for a size similar to the Bull Terrier, 15 to 18 inches (38 to 46 cm), but breeders were producing Staffies who were too heavy and clumsy. By 1948, the standard called for a diminished size of 14 to 16 inches (36 to 41 cm), although many Staffy breeders balked at this change.

The Modern-Day Staffy in the UK

The modern Staffy is an energetic, intelligent, and handsome dog who ranges from 14 to 16 inches (36 to 41 cm) tall and weighs no more than 40 pounds (18 kg). According to Kennel

Staffy "Firsts"

- The very first Staffy club show took place in August 1935, in Cradley Heath, Midlands, England. The first championships were earned in 1938 by Staffies born and bred in the Midlands, Ch. Gentleman Jim and Ch. Lady Eve.
- The first Staffy registered with the AKC was Wheeler's Black Dinah, in 1936.
- The first Staffy to win an AKC championship was Maher's Captain D, in 1937.

Club registrations, the Staffy is currently one of the top ten most popular breeds in Great Britain. The English publication *K9 Magazine* ran a comparison of dog breeds, scoring each on a variety of quantifiable, important factors: broad appeal/popularity and availability, average life expectancy, hereditary illness (eye problems), insurance, feeding costs, and maintenance. By virtue of this ranking, the Staffy was rated the world's best dog breed.

BREED HISTORY IN THE US

The history of the United States itself is young, so it follows that the Staffy's presence here is relatively new. Irish and English industrial immigrants made their way to American shores in the late seventeenth century to work in the mines, bringing their Bulldog-terrier mixes with them.

Dog Fighting in the New World

Dog fighting in the New World soon became as popular and prevalent as in Europe; American pioneers found it as great a diversion from the tedium of daily life as their British counterparts had. They, too, took notice of the Bull-and-Terrier's admirable traits and started to develop their own bloodlines, keeping meticulous records. The new and improved dogs became well known outside of the fighting ring for their strong, handsome physical appearance and their loving, loyal dispositions within their families.

The Road to Recognition

The new dogs were first called by several different names: Yankee Terriers, American Bull Terriers, and American (Pit) Bull Terriers. Even then, the word "pit" was apparently an undesirable component of a breed name, but parentheses around the word didn't change the disturbing truth about these dogs' fighting history. This was emphasized by the AKC's refusal to accept the "pit bull" dogs for registration, wanting to disassociate itself from any breed commonly identified with blood sports. This prejudice, however well intended, spurred the creation of a new registry. The United Kennel Club (UKC) was founded in 1898, specifically for the breed ultimately known as the American Pit Bull Terrier (APBT), but it opened its doors to all dog breeds.

In an effort to eradicate the unsavory fighting associations with the word "pit," the AKC decided to admit a breed called the American Staffordshire Terrier (AmStaff). This dog was virtually identical to the APBT but carried a name that distinguished it from its bloody origins. The word "bull" was also dropped from this breed's name to avoid confusion with the British version known as the Staffordshire Bull Terrier (Staffy). There were now three similar yet distinct breeds of the original dog: the American Staffordshire Terrier, the American Pit Bull Terrier, and the Staffordshire Bull Terrier.

Timeline in the United States

1936: The first Staffordshire Bull Terrier Club of America is organized.

1972: The breed name officially becomes "Staffordshire Bull Terrier" after the Staffordshire Terrier breed splits into two breeds: the American Staffordshire Terrier and the Staffordshire Bull Terrier.

1974: The AKC recognizes the Staffordshire Bull Terrier.

Because of the confusion that naturally ensued, Staffy fanciers wanted to make sure that their breed did not fade into oblivion. The first Staffordshire Terrier Club of America was founded in 1936 to protect "the Grand Old

With his shorter legs and stockier body, the Staffordshire Bull Terrier (left) is quite distinctive from the American Pit Bull Terrier (middle) and American Staffordshire Terrier (right).

Breed." The breed standard was immediately compiled, and the first Staffordshire Terriers entered American show rings. The word "bull" didn't officially reappear as part of the breed's name in United States registries until 1972.

The Modern-Day Staffy in the US

In 1974, the Staffordshire Bull Terrier became an AKC-recognized breed, using the same breed name employed by Joe Dunn in England in the 1930s. Whereas the APBT and the AmStaff are so similar in appearance that it's hard to tell them apart, the Staffy's look is distinctive, with his shorter legs and stockier body. There is no marked difference between the Staffy bred in the US and the Staffy bred in the UK. They both adhere to the same breed standard: a size that ranges from 14 to 16 inches (36 to 41 cm) tall and no more than 40 pounds (18 kg) in weight.

According to current AKC registration statistics, the Staffy is in the top hundred most popular breeds in the United States. It may take a few more years for the Staffy Bull's popularity in the United States to catch up with that in Great Britain, but the "nanny dog" will no doubt win America over.

Celebrity Staffy Owners

Linda Blair
Frankie Muñoz
Carson Palmer (of the Cincinnati Bengals)
Ray Romano
Arnold Vosloo
Richard Zanuck (son of movie mogul Darryl Zanuck)

CHARACTERISTICS

of the Staffordshire Bull Terrier

espite the bloody history of the "bully breeds," there is no denying the fact that the Staffordshire Bull Terrier has many wonderful qualities that make him a perfect companion. The power and tenacity that created such a stir in the dog-fighting world still exist, but these traits no longer define the breed. Today, the Staffy is known not just for his handsome physique and strong constitution but for his unending fondness for children and loyalty to his human family. It might seem contradictory, but the very qualities that made the dog a good fighter are the same ones that make him a great lover; they're simply channeled in a positive way.

THE BREED STANDARD

The official description of the way a particular dog should look and conduct himself is called the breed standard and is the ideal against which all dogs of that breed are measured. Show dogs in conformation are all judged by how closely they compare to the breed standard. Show champions come very close to this perfection, which is why they become desirable as stud dogs or brood bitches.

The following section is based on the American Kennel Club (AKC) standard for the breed. Keep in mind that the standard describes the "ideal" Staffy Bull—dogs who deviate from the standard can still make wonderful pets.

General Appearance

The Staffordshire Bull Terrier is a medium-sized dog with an average life span of 11 or 12 years. He has a stocky, muscular build with a broad head, thick neck, powerful jaws, a somewhat short snout, and short, floppy ears. This sturdy, solid dog also should be playful, energetic, and agile. Even when standing still, the ideal Staffy cuts an impressive figure.

Size, Proportion, Substance

A Staffy's height at the shoulder should measure 14 to 16 inches (36 to 41 cm). A

The Staffordshire Bull Terrier is a medium-sized dog with a stocky, muscular build.

male should weigh between 28 to 38 pounds (13 to 17 kg), and a female should weigh 24 to 34 pounds (11 to 15 kg). Height and weight should be proportional. Generally speaking, the length of the dog's back (from withers to tail set) should be equal to the distance measured from the withers to the ground.

Head

The head offers the first impression of a dog's overall appearance and should present a chiseled look. The head also should have a distinct stop, short foreface, and a black nose. A pink, or Dudley, nose is considered a serious fault. A Staffy's nose is more elongated than that of his Bulldog or Boxer cousins, which makes breathing easier. Pendulous jowls, considered a detriment in the fighting pit, were bred out during dog fighting's heyday.

Eyes

Dark is preferable but may bear some relation to coat color.

What Is a Breed Standard?

Every recognized dog breed has a standardized list of specific physical and temperamental requirements that an ideal dog of that breed should possess. The official standard is written by the parent club of each breed and serves as a blueprint against which all dogs shown in conformation are judged. While a judge's interpretation of a contestant's adherence to the breed standard may be subjective in some respects, the standard's goal is to emphasize the most important aspects of the dog. Standards may vary from registry to registry and from country to country. Occasionally, a club will make changes to the breed standard that must be voted on and formally adopted. The AKC standard for the Staffy was most recently adopted on January 1, 1990.

Eyes should be round and medium sized, and set to look straight ahead. Light-colored eyes or pink eye rims are considered faults, except when the coat color surrounding the eye is white. In this case, pink eye rims are allowed.

Mouth

The outer side of the lower incisors should touch the inner side of the upper incisors to form a "scissors" bite. Lips should be tight and clean. A badly undershot or overshot bite is considered a serious fault.

Ears

The ears should be rose set (meaning they should be small and set high on the skull, with the flap opening out and lying slightly backward, resembling an open rose) or half pricked and not of a large size. Full drop or full prick ears are considered a serious fault. Cropped ears are not allowed.

Neck, Topline, Body

The neck is rather short and muscular, clean in outline and widening toward the shoulders. The Staffy's body has a level topline and is close-coupled, meaning there is little space between the ribcage and the hindquarters, contributing to the Staffy's short, stocky appearance. The chest is wide and deep, sometimes called a "barrel

The Staffy's neck is short and muscular, clean in outline, and widening toward the shoulders.

Ear Cropping

Ear cropping is a controversial subject around the world because no medical reason exists for it. There is no truth behind the theory that cropped ears are less susceptible to ear afflictions than natural ears. In dog fighting days, ears were cropped to give the dog a fiercer look and to eliminate the risk of ear injury. Natural ears were too easy a jaw-hold for the pit opponent, and ripped ears bled profusely.

Today, the practice of ear cropping is outlawed in several countries, England among them. Because the Staffy breed standard calls for natural ears that are rose set or half pricked, there is no need to subject your Staffy to this surgical ordeal. If you want to show a Staffy whose natural ears are too floppy to meet the breed standard, partial ear cropping is a possible solution. Make sure, however, that you have the procedure performed by a veterinarian who is not only experienced with ear cropping but familiar with the desired look of a Staffy.

chest." Ribs should be well sprung and the body tapered to a lean loin area. The tail is medium length, set and carried low on the body, without a curl. It tapers to a point and should not be docked.

Forequarters

The front legs should be straight and well boned, set rather far apart, with the feet turning out slightly. There should be no looseness at the shoulders and no weakness at the pasterns or "wrists." The dewclaws may be removed, but there is no requirement to do so.

Feet should be well padded, strong, and medium sized.

Hindquarters

The back legs should be well muscled, with hocks, or rear "ankles," let down (meaning the hock joints are relatively close

The Staffy's coat should be smooth, short, and close to the skin.

to the ground, making the hocks short or "let down"). Short hocks indicate greater stability and strength. The stifles, or "knees," should be well bent. When viewed from behind, the legs should appear parallel. Dewclaws on the hind legs, if any, are usually removed. The feet should turn out slightly.

Coat

The Staffy coat should be smooth, short, and close to the skin. No trimming of the coat or whiskers is permitted. The hair should be glossy and lie flat.

Color

Staffies may be red, fawn, white, black, blue, or any of these colors with white, known as "flash." Brindle (a tiger-like striping pattern) and flashy brindle are acceptable. The only disqualifying colors are liver or black and tan.

Gait

The Staffy's gait should be free, powerful, and agile, without excess effort. Legs should move parallel when viewed from the front or the rear. Hind legs should show a discernible drive, meaning that the back legs should appear powerful enough to provide propulsion from the rear.

Temperament

You can expect a Staffy to be protective, curious, and loving. Although every dog is an individual with variations in personality, certain traits are common to all dogs. Young Staffy pups love to chew and should be constantly provided with acceptable alternatives to your furniture, books, and children's toys. Their toughness of build and robust activity level make them ideal tug-of-war partners! Remember, though, that with any kind of roughhouse play, your dog must always know that you are in charge and you set the tone for play. Whether keeping a watchful eye on the children of the family or chasing a ball around the yard, there's no doubt that the "nanny dog" lives each day to the fullest.

As much as Staffies love their people, their affections don't usually extend to other dogs. It's not uncommon for a Staffy puppy to tolerate or even play with a strange dog, but don't

What's a Dewclaw?

A dewclaw is an extra claw within a toe placed high on the pastern; it has no purpose, as the toe placement is too high to contact the ground when the dog is moving. Consequently, the dewclaw is never worn down naturally and must be kept short. Long dewclaws can catch on outdoor obstacles, such as tree roots, and cause a serious, painful injury to the dog. Most breeders and dog owners have the dewclaws removed when puppies are very young, eliminating the risk of injury altogether.

expect the same reaction from an adult Staffy.

Staffies enjoy creature comforts as much as we do, and it's not unusual to see one selecting the softest part of the rug to relax on, stretching his back legs out full length behind him. They've also been known to sit up on their haunches with their back legs splayed in a "V" shape.

It's important to remember that a Staffy's comical, sociable nature comes with a need to be with the people he loves. One of the surest ways to make your Staffy miserable is to make him live apart from the family, tied up or restricted by himself to the yard or doghouse. If you're not willing to accept the Staffy as a full-fledged member of the family, you're not ready to own a dog.

IS A STAFFY RIGHT FOR YOU?

Adding a pet to the family is a decision that should not be made lightly. Dogs are social, sentient creatures who deserve the comforts of a good home for the duration of their lives. Too often, puppies are taken home on a whim or because a child has just seen *Lady and the Tramp* or *101 Dalmatians*, with no research into the breed or thought given to the demands and restrictions a pet can make on a person's life. Many a Dalmatian has been given over to a shelter because the family was unprepared for the cute puppy from the movies to grow into a big dog who isn't particularly good with children. The first important step to adding a dog to the family is to carefully examine your lifestyle and decide whether he fits into that lifestyle.

Once you've decided that you're ready for a dog and have your heart set on a Staffy, it's time to do more homework. As wonderful a pet as the Staffy makes, the breed has inherent qualities that can be problematic, as does every breed. For instance, the Staffy's natural intolerance for other dogs means that he's not the ideal breed to bring into a family with dogs already established in the pack hierarchy, and his need to be with his family a lot can pose a dilemma for two adults working long hours away from home.

However, the Staffy makes an appealing pet for many reasons. He requires minimal grooming, is loving and loyal, and fits in well with most family situations. But you must ask yourself some important questions before bringing home a Staffy to make sure that everyone's needs will be met. Dog ownership comes with responsibility to your dog, your family, and your community. If you aren't prepared to meet those responsibilities head on and with an open heart, reconsider your decision altogether.

Children

The Staffy's reputation as the "nanny dog" makes him a natural choice for a family with children. A people-lover in general, the Staffy has a special affinity for children and instinctively knows when to be protective, when to be playful, and when to be extra gentle.

As with any breed of dog you add to your family, it's important that children are old enough to understand how a puppy or dog must be treated. Babies and toddlers may have affectionate intentions, but their idea of a gentle pat on the head often translates into a hearty *thwack*. Although a Staffy will stoically endure overzealous shows of affection, a young puppy may not understand and may become frightened. Careful supervision is necessary whenever children and dogs are together.

The Staffy is often referred to as the "nanny dog" because of his natural affinity for children.

For post-toddler-age children, adding a dog to the family is a good opportunity to teach them about respect and gentle handling of animals in general. Here again, constant supervision is mandatory. If you decide to acquire a puppy rather than an adult dog, you might find the demands of puppyhood a bit overwhelming when combined with the demands of parenting very young children. It may be best for everyone to wait until the kids are mature enough to understand a puppy's needs.

Children and Dogs

Before adding a dog to the family, one of the most important breed characteristics to consider is your desired breed's compatibility with children. If you have youngsters at home, it is pointlessly risky to obtain a breed with little tolerance for children's loud play and sometimes overzealous attentions. Fortunately, the Staffy is not merely good with children, he is naturally fond and protective of them. While play between children and pets should always be supervised, it's no accident that the Staffy is called the "nanny dog!"

Environment

Where you live has a direct impact on any dog you add to the family, so it's important to evaluate your living situation and its suitability for a dog.

City Living

Healthy Staffies are athletic, energetic dogs who need regular, vigorous exercise. They won't be happy, nor is it fair to coop them up in a city apartment all day, with no significant diversion. City-dwelling Staffies should have, at minimum, a family member, friend, or professional dog walker come over at least twice during a business day to provide social interaction and take the dog for a walk to relieve himself. If you use a dog walker, find out if she will be taking other "clients" for a walk at the same time. A Staffy may not harmoniously share his walk with other dogs.

Most cities have parks that offer a taste of the countryside to urban residents, but before you take your Staffy there for a romp, find out if pets are welcome. If so, what are the rules? If there is a designated area where dogs can be off leash to play, remember that the Staffy isn't always tolerant of other dogs. Even if yours is very well trained and behaves perfectly, you really can't vouch for the other dogs in the park. The last thing you want is an altercation.

Rural Living

If you live in a rural area, a Staffy should fit well into your home. He needs room to run and romp, and what could be better than a nice backyard? Of course, the yard or designated play area should be fenced in for the dog's safety and your own peace of mind. The fence should be high enough so that the dog can't jump over it to escape—although with a determined Staffy, anything is possible—and set deeply enough into the ground so that he can't dig his way out. For extra security, some homeowners add a barrier beneath the ground where the fence is set to prevent the Great Escape.

Suburban Living

If you live in the suburbs but don't have a suitable yard or exercise area for a dog, be prepared to take long walks! The energetic Staffy requires rigorous activity. Not only is exercise important for his physical health, it is crucial to his mental well-being. Without sufficient exercise, a Staffy will become bored and depressed. He will go looking for something to occupy himself, which usually leads to mischievous and/or destructive behavior. A healthy adult Staffy who doesn't have a large area in which to romp should go on a nice long walk of at least 2 miles (3 km), weather permitting. Of course, you wouldn't want to subject him or yourself to extreme temperatures or conditions, but the bottom line is that if you haven't the time or appropriate place to keep a Staffy well exercised, consider a different breed.

Exercise

The Staffy is an athletic, vital dog who requires regular, hardcore exercise. Not only is it an outlet for his natural exuberance, it's important to his physical and mental well-being. Without sufficient exercise, a Staffy can become bored and depressed. Bored dogs can become destructive in their quest for something to occupy them.

Dog Walks

The type of exercise your Staffy needs may not be compatible with your lifestyle, so it's important to evaluate what type of physical activity you can offer a Staffy. If you live in an apartment, will you or someone else be able to take him on regular walks at least twice a day? A brief stroll around the

The Staffy is an athletic dog who requires regular, vigorous exercise.

block may take care of a Staffy's elimination needs but doesn't do much to contribute to his daily exercise quota. A vigorous leash walk of a couple of miles (km) suits the healthy adult Staffy much better, provided the walker is strong enough to control the dog if he starts to pull. The Staffy is stronger than his small stature suggests and could easily prove no match for the child or fragile senior citizen at the other end of the leash. His regular walker should be of sufficient stamina to keep up with a Staffy on walks. The exercise will benefit both.

Playtime

It's unlikely that a dog will entertain himself for any significant length of time by running around even a spacious yard or penned-in exercise area. Moreover, the Staffy is a very social breed who thrives on the companionship of his humans. He won't be content to frolic in the yard by himself while you and the family are inside. It's preferable to play an active game of ball or flying disc with him, meeting both his physical and emotional needs.

When you just can't break away to play with your Staffy, try providing some kind of permanent diversion in his outdoor

Is a Staffy Right for You?

Staffy ownership is not for everybody. Before you commit to adding one to your family, ask yourself these questions:

- *Am I willing to be a Staffy ambassador?* This esoteric breed is not widely known or seen in the US, so people may automatically conclude that your Staffy is either a "pit bull" in general or an AmStaff or APBT in particular. This is your chance to introduce Americans to the wonderful breed so well known in the UK. Moreover, it's an opportunity to educate the public about the differences in bully breeds and the propaganda that still surrounds them. You should be willing to answer the many questions asked of you whenever you and your Staffy do the town.

- *Do I have the resources needed to invest in the socialization and training of a Staffy?* A dog is a lifetime investment, financially, physically, and emotionally. You may be the most eager would-be Staffy owner in the world, but if you don't earn enough money to pay for the care he should receive during the decade or so of his lifetime, rethink the feasibility of adding one to your family. The active, intelligent Staffy requires thorough socialization and training if he hopes to prove that he's not the vicious demon "pit bulls" are thought to be. Be prepared to invest time and money in the endeavor.

- *Can I afford to buy a top-quality Staffy?* When it comes to this breed, you don't want a bargain-basement dog with a dubious background, especially if you're a first-time Staffy owner. He is too powerful to behave unpredictably, even if you diligently set out to train him. The extra money you'll pay an experienced, reputable Staffy breeder will be well spent in knowing he's been temperament and health tested.

- *Have I thoroughly researched the breed and evaluated my suitability as a Staffy owner?* If you've done your homework and believe that both your family and your Staffy will benefit from sharing life with one another, "bully" for you! You're in for a great ride.

area, like an old tire hanging by a rope or a tetherball, although it's still likely that he will show more interest in being indoors with you instead of playing outside by himself. Ideally, a Staffy owner will have the time and ability to devote to her dog on a daily basis.

The Staffy is a very social breed who enjoys playing outside with his humans.

Dog Sports

Another excellent physical activity for your Staffy is an organized dog sport, like agility or flyball. These types of pursuits provide a fun, interactive way to exercise your dog, along with the challenge of competition. Both sports award titles but include the hard exercise that competitive conformation and obedience don't. Your Staffy will love the chance to show off his intelligence and athleticism. Contact your local Staffy club for information on organized sports in your area.

Grooming Needs

When deciding on what breed of dog is right for you, grooming needs should be near the top of your list of considerations. Some people have no problem with the time and money required to keep certain high-maintenance breeds well groomed. But if you're looking for a breed that's more the wash-and-wear type, the Staffy is for you.

The Staffy's grooming requirements are neither time consuming nor costly. He is naturally a clean dog whose short coat rarely requires bathing and needs only a minimum of brushing. His fur does shed, but it won't be in the same volume as it is for longer-haired breeds like the Keeshond or Siberian Husky.

Brushing

Regular brushing will remove dead hair and condition a dog's skin by distributing the natural oils in his coat, affording better protection from the elements. When he sheds profusely between seasons, a shedding comb is useful for removing the dead undercoat that sloughs off to make way for new growth. In addition to keeping your Staffy looking his best, regular brushing can be a pleasant bonding opportunity for the two of you. After all, brushing a short-haired dog like the Staffy is really a form of petting, and he'll readily come to enjoy grooming sessions.

Bathing

Frequent bathing of your Staffy is not needed and not recommended. He won't require a bath unless he's rolled in mud or gotten into some other type of irresistible muck. Regular brushing and a healthful diet are all your Staffy needs to keep his skin and coat shiny and fresh smelling. Excessive bathing strips natural oils that condition the dog's skin and hair and can lead to itchy, uncomfortable skin or other dermatological ailments. If you feel strongly about bathing your dog on a regular basis, keep it down to once a month, using a specially formulated dog shampoo. Human soap, shampoos, and body washes often contain some kind of detergent and are too harsh for a dog's skin. Keep him out of drafts and cold temperatures until he's thoroughly dry, then watch that Staffy shine!

Other Pets

Like his "bully breed" relatives, the Staffy's natural love for and friendliness toward humans doesn't always extend to other pets in the home. The Staffy has a certain amount of dog aggression in his genetic composition, but that doesn't mean that he can't live happily in a multi-pet home. With careful, diligent socialization and training, a Staffy may be able to live in harmony with other Staffies and dog breeds. When possible, the newest dog added to the family should be of the opposite sex to minimize the aggression and dominance issues that can spring up between same-sex dogs.

Dog and Dog

Introducing the new dog and the established dog should take place on neutral turf to prevent territorial behavior. Both dogs should be leashed but allowed to sniff and greet each other as much as they like. Never leave a new puppy alone with an established pet dog until you are confident of their compatibility. Eventually, one of the dogs should emerge as the dominant one—and it won't necessarily be the older or more established of the two. Once in a while, though, competition for the alpha role can continue unresolved. This is a sad situation that may require permanent separation of the dogs within the home. In some cases, a suitable new home for one of them may be the only recourse.

Although the Staffy has a certain amount of dog aggression in his genetic composition, lots of socialization and training may enable him to live in harmony with other canines.

Dog and Cat

Introducing a Staffy pup to the family cat should be conducted tactfully. Cats will usually resent an interloper and keep their distance until they accept the fact that the stranger is

Staffordshire Bull Terrier Myths

Myth: The breed is just one of those horrible "pit bulls."

Truth: There is no such breed as a "pit bull." The Staffy is one of several breeds descended from dogs used in the cruel entertainment of animal baiting and fighting, but this is not tantamount to a naturally vicious nature or aggression toward humans.

Myth: The Staffy's sweet disposition makes him a natural playmate for other dogs.

Truth: Given the breed's unsavory fighting history, it shouldn't be surprising that the Staffy has a certain tendency toward dog aggression and should not be placed in a situation where this aggression can manifest.

Myth: The Staffy is a dangerous breed that should be legally banned.

Truth: Societal stigmas against various breeds have come and gone, as we've seen with Rottweilers and Doberman Pinschers. Hollywood often perpetuates misconceptions with its portrayal of certain dogs in certain ways, as with the rise in Dalmatian purchases after the movie *101 Dalmatians* was released. Unfortunately, only after relenting to their children's pleas to get one of these cuddly, spotty dogs did parents find out that Dalmatians are not especially compatible with kids. Animal shelters were bursting with Dalmatians given away by these impulsive buyers. The fact is that any dog, regardless of breed, who isn't socialized or properly trained can be a threat to society. Breed-specific legislation unfairly targets certain breeds and does nothing to prevent attacks on humans.

Myth: Staffies make good watch dogs.

Truth: The Staffy was not developed to be a true guard dog. The tenacious, fearless pit fighter of yesteryear wouldn't have lifted a paw to protect his handler's home from intruders. He likes people too well! A burglar breaking into a Staffy's home is more likely to be greeted with kisses than with growls. He will alert his family to the approach of visitors and is instinctively protective of his humans, but the Staffy just isn't aggressive enough to safeguard belongings.

Myth: The Staffy has jaws that lock.

Truth: This misconception arises from the fighting Staffy's unusual gameness and tenacity in the pit. No physiological ability exists to lock a Staffy's jaws in place.

there to stay. The first time you introduce your new puppy to your cat, defer to the latter's rank by holding onto the pup, not the cat. Some cats and dogs become best friends, while others will merely tolerate each other. In some cases, they will stay away from each other as much as possible. You can only do so much to foster harmony, and let nature handle the rest.

Dog and Small Pets

Small pets like rodents or reptiles should be kept away from dogs and cats, who are their natural predators. On television, we see the occasional video clip of a pet bird bonding with the family dog, but it's more the exception than the rule. If you already have multiple pets in the home, think twice before adding a Staffy to the mix. After all, the Staffy is a terrier whose instinct is to track small animals like rodents. Such a change to the "pack" dynamic should be in the best interest of all the family pets.

Protective Instincts

Don't let the Staffy's small stature fool you. Despite his affectionate disposition, the Staffy's very appearance and presentation make him an effective watchdog by default. He isn't likely to attack anyone approaching the home, even an "uninvited guest," but he will surely announce the arrival! A Staffy will bark excitedly to welcome a visitor, even one with criminal intent—but an intruder won't hang around to find out

Because the Staffy is so social, he needs lots of time and attention from his owner.

Staffies and Human Aggression

A properly bred and trained Staffy should not display any aggression toward humans, so what's with those news items on yet another child mauled by a "pit bull?" The fact is that the dog in question probably isn't a pure Staffy but some untrained "bully breed" mix. Or he might not have any "bully breed" in him at all but is dubbed a "pit bull" by overanxious reporters pursuing a sensational story. A Schnauzer who bites a child isn't usually considered news—a "pit bull" is.

if this impressive-looking powerhouse is friendly or not. Although not bred with protection in mind, as are the Doberman Pinscher and the Bullmastiff, the athletic, loyal Staffy can be a fearless force to reckon with, especially if he senses a threat to his humans.

Schedule

Do you live alone and work full time? If so, Staffy ownership presents its own challenges. Dogs, by nature, are pack animals who thrive in a social environment. So how does a single adult working outside of the home provide the attention and care a companion dog—especially a Staffy—needs? By recognizing that extra effort is required. You may come home at the end of your workday tired, wanting nothing more than to collapse on the sofa with a TV dinner, but a responsible Staffy owner knows that her dog's needs come first. You owe it to your dog to spend some quality time walking, feeding, and just interacting with him once you arrive home. If work delays you, you'll need to call on a trusted friend or neighbor with whom you've arranged to ensure that your Staffy has dinner and a potty break. If possible, hiring a dog walker to take your Staffy out in the middle of the day will satisfy his elimination and socializing needs until his favorite human comes home from work.

Full-time working people are sometimes able to bring their dogs to work with them. A self-employed person or member of a small, pet-friendly office could possibly take a Staffy to work every day. It's not unheard of for mental health professionals in the right setting to allow their patients to interact with the "office dog." As we know, dogs can be very comforting when we are in distress. Similarly, shop owners may bring their well-trained dogs to work, knowing the pets are only too happy to be with their humans and feel included.

Trainability

One of the Staffy's most endearing traits is the high intelligence that makes him such an entertaining and rewarding breed with which to interact. Sometimes, though, the price of this cleverness is a tendency toward stubbornness and independence, traits that can prove challenging to the Staffy trainer. On the flip side, such a smart dog is quick to pick up on what you want him to do. If you practice patience and persistence, he will allow his desire to please you overcome any resistance he may feel.

Staffies tend to mimic the behavior they observe from their owners. This means that if you take a Staffy into a large, boisterous family, he is likely to exhibit high energy and want to join in family activities. If he is brought into a quiet home of just adults with one or two older children, he will take his cue from them and be content to hang out and relax with the family. This doesn't dispel his need for exercise; rather, it governs his overall behavior. And a calm, thoroughly exercised dog is much more receptive and responsive to obedience training.

The decision to purchase or adopt a Staffy is not one to be taken lightly. You should be prepared to give your all as caretaker, trainer, playmate, and protector. Anything less is unfair to the dog. But you can be sure that, when you do invest the love and care he deserves, the dividends you reap will be priceless.

PREPARING

for Your Staffordshire Bull Terrier

The decision to make a dog part of your family is an important one, and preparation for his arrival should be treated with equal care and thoroughness. After all, you wouldn't bring home a newborn baby from the hospital without first stocking up on necessities like diapers and formula. Preparation for your new Staffy, whether puppy or adult, requires similar attention.

INITIAL CONSIDERATIONS

Before you get your heart set on adding a Staffy to your family, make sure that you're not faced with any legislative obstacles. Unfortunately, some areas do have legal restrictions on ownership and/or residency of so-called "vicious" breeds. The list of these breeds varies from place to place but typically includes all breeds related to—or even just physically resembling—the nebulous "pit bull." This means that the American Pit Bull Terrier, the American Staffordshire Terrier, the Staffordshire Bull Terrier, the American Bulldog, the Bull Terrier, and even sometimes the Boxer and the (English) Bulldog are deemed "dangerous" breeds that fall under the umbrella of such legislation. Far worse than the unfair legislation precluding the addition of a Staffy to your family is the Staffy who is confiscated from an unsuspecting new owner and ends up in a shelter or euthanized.

Once you get the green light to purchase or adopt a Staffy, take time to look at the big picture and clarify your expectations for your pet. Do you want a companion to accompany the family on outings? Do you want an exceptionally trustworthy pet for your children who have been pleading for a dog? Do you want your dog to participate in organized activities for dogs, or more specifically, for Staffies? Do you prefer one gender over the other? If so, are there any gender-specific traits you need to be aware of? Do you plan to become involved with the breeding community yourself? These are all valid points that warrant consideration. Once you have a clear vision of life with your Staffy, you will be better equipped to select the right dog from the right source.

Before purchasing or adopting a Staffy, research your area's laws regarding the breed.

Puppy Versus Adult

Once you commit to adding a Staffy to your household, the next question is whether to get a puppy or adult dog.

Puppies

Most people tend to prefer puppies, and who can blame them? Few creatures in this world are more endearing. Yet bringing home a puppy presents its own unique preparations and commitments. You must be mentally and pragmatically ready to deal with housetraining, teething, puppy-proofing your home, and practicing patience during the pup's transition from communal littermate to independent pet.

A puppy is virtually a clean slate with no previous ownership and no bad habits to unlearn. You get to establish the boundaries for his life with you. This means that you're responsible for the puppy's training, and the reward is a Staffy who lives in harmony with your family. The joys of puppyhood amply compensate for the high-maintenance phase, but it's not for everyone. If you don't think you can handle the stress of the first few weeks, think about whether an adult may be better for you.

Adults

What if you'd rather skip the work and disruption involved in raising a puppy? First, pat yourself on the back for your honesty. There is no point in making yourself miserable and shortchanging the puppy if your heart isn't in it. There is no shame in adopting an adult Staffy or older "youngster" who would be a better fit for you.

An adult dog may be a good choice for a senior citizen or someone with health limitations that preclude the physical exertions necessary in rearing a puppy. Many adult dogs adopted into new homes are already housetrained. If your

Laws Surrounding Your Staffy

The pet population has escalated to the extent where many states, cities, and municipalities have enacted legislation that regulates pet ownership, care, and even how the pet is permitted to interact with society. For Staffies, this legislation can have major implications, so check on any legislation that is in place where you live prior to adding a Staffy to the family.

Breed-Specific Legislation

Laws against certain breeds deemed "vicious" are in effect in many parts of the country to prohibit the ownership of applicable breeds. Unfortunately, this kind of law doesn't deter ownership by the unscrupulous people whom it targets; instead, it makes life difficult for responsible dog owners who only want to do right by their dogs and their community. This type of misapplied legislation impacts not only Staffies but any of the bully breeds descended from ancient fighting dogs. These include the American Pit Bull Terrier, the American Staffordshire Terrier, the Bull Terrier, the Bulldog, and others. Even a dog of uncertain origin who physically or temperamentally resembles one of the bully breeds can be subject to these laws. If you live with a Staffy in one of these areas, be aware that your dog can legally be confiscated and destroyed, even if he's done nothing perceived as controversial, such as inciting dog aggression, growling at a human, or jumping up on a human.

Before you get a Staffy or move with your Staffy to a new location, check into these laws and spare your family possible heartbreak later on.

Leash Laws

Just about every community has a law requiring pet dogs to be leashed in public. This may seem unfair if your dog is perfectly trained and obedient, but it is really for his safety. Pedestrians and bicyclists can have an accident while trying to avoid collision with a loose dog. By keeping him on a leash, you protect your Staffy and other people from injury. Don't give anyone an excuse to report your Staffy by disregarding leash laws.

Licensing Laws

While checking for breed-specific legislation in your area, you should also check into dog licensing requirements. Many areas require pets to be officially registered. You'll receive a tag, similar to your Staffy's rabies vaccination tag, with the county or city name and a registration number. The fee you pay for this license is money well spent because it essentially provides a registry that may come in handy if your dog is ever lost. Licensing also helps local government keep accurate records on the pet population to ensure that the necessary animal control services are provided.

"No Pet" Policies

Unfortunately, many shelter dogs are given up because an owner is moving to a place that doesn't allow pets. Apartment dwellers must be aware of this frequent rule. Sometimes a compassionate landlady may be persuaded to let you move in with your dog. A well-mannered, clean, likeable dog can be his own best argument for permission to live there. You will probably be asked to make a deposit against any damage to the dwelling, which may or may not be refundable when you move out. Some buildings and rental homes may allow only certain pets—cats but not dogs or dogs under a certain size—so be sure to ask for specifics. Above all, never cause a landlady to regret her decision to allow your Staffy in the building.

Waste Clean-Up Laws

Some people do not obey these laws, as we all see by the random piles out there. But imagine what our sidewalks and streets would look like if this legislation didn't exist. It doesn't take a lot of time or effort to pick up after your Staffy, and fancy contraptions don't work any better than an ordinary plastic grocery bag. Insert your hand into the bag and pick up the stool. Turn the bag inside out, tie it up, and you have done the job without your hands touching the waste. If you dislike the feel of physically picking up the stool, many types of poop-scooping aids are on the market. Check your local pet supply store for rake-and-shovel tools or self-closing, biodegradable bags.

lifestyle doesn't afford you the large chunks of time you'd need to spend with a new puppy, adopting a homeless adult Staffy who is accustomed to being on his own may be a perfect solution. Or if you have young children who don't yet understand the special handling puppies require, a more stoic, low-key adult dog makes an appropriate pet. Above all, remember that cute puppies rarely have difficulty finding homes, but adult dogs can spend longer periods of time in shelters, hoping for a placement. Providing a loving, safe new environment for a homeless adult dog is a selfless gift of compassion. Many times these dogs are aware of their good fortune and reward adoptive parents with impeccable manners, cheerful dispositions, and years of unconditional love.

Finding a healthy adult purebred Staffy is challenging but not impossible. Chances are you won't happen on one at the local animal shelter. Most shelter dogs are mixed breeds, although pure breeds are sometimes released to shelters. It never hurts to try, though. You can put in a request for a Staffy should one come into the shelter's ranks of adoptable dogs.

A more likely source for an adoptable adult Staffy is a reputable breeder. Sometimes breeders have more adults than they feel they can afford to care for, especially if the dog isn't breeding stock or has already borne several litters. Usually, nothing is mentally or physically wrong with these dogs; the breeder just wants them in homes where they can get the individualized attention they deserve.

Yet another plan for adopting an adult Staffy is a rescue program. Most breeds have their own regional rescue organizations that remove dogs of any age from abusive and/or neglectful homes. The rescued dogs go to foster homes until permanent loving homes can be found for them. In the Staffy's case, as with all bully breeds, a dog who has been trained to fight or encouraged to behave aggressively as a status symbol for a misguided owner may come to a rescue organization. These dogs require very special new owners, willing and able to go through rehabilitation. Sadly, some dogs rescued from illegal fighting rings are so unpredictable that they are considered unfit for adoption and must be euthanized.

An adult dog—regardless of circumstances—may come with issues of his own. Learn as much as you possibly can about an adult Staffy's background before accepting him. For the patient new owner, most issues can be overcome with time and love, and one more homeless dog may be saved from euthanasia.

Male Versus Female

Ask Staffy owners which sex your new pet should be and you will get a variety of opinions. Some people swear that females are more easily trained and form closer emotional bonds with their owners. Others firmly believe that males have more character and more consistent temperaments. When all is said and done, personality is subjective and varies from dog to dog. Gender is merely a matter of preference or even the luck of the draw. You may plan to view a litter of available Staffies and lay claim to whichever puppy steals your heart…or chooses you!

Remember that, regardless of gender, you should alter (spay or neuter) your new Staffy unless you plan to breed or show the dog in conformation. Not only will this prevent the birth of

Color Me Happy

Staffies come in a wide variety of colors, but color shouldn't be your primary concern when choosing a puppy. Health and temperament are just as important, if not more so. After all, there's really no such thing as an unattractive Staffy!

A dog's personality is subjective and varies from dog to dog.

37

more unwanted puppies in an already overpopulated world, but there are advantages for the owner. By removing the sexual hormones and accompanying tensions, you will spare yourself the inconvenience of twice yearly estrus cycles ("heat") in females and the determined, more dominating nature of intact males. If you opt not to alter your pet Staffy, remember that you leave the female dog open to potential health issues such as false pregnancy and uterine cancer. Or your intact male may have a tendency to roam, requiring extra-vigilant supervision. When it comes to training the intact male, be ready to practice extra patience. Discuss the subject with your breeder or vet.

Show Dog Versus Pet-Quality Dog

As you research Staffy breeders, you will no doubt discover that they may have varying prices for puppies of the same litter. Pups deemed show quality are more expensive than their pet-quality littermates, often with no discernible difference to the potential owner's eye. The lower price in no way represents an unhealthy or otherwise defective puppy; it simply indicates that the pet-quality pup will not grow into a dog suitable for conformation showing. He may have feet that turn out a wee bit more than the breed standard permits or black-and-tan or liver coloring that is unacceptable in the show ring. Physiological deviations from the breed standard don't portend future health problems, only that the dog doesn't sufficiently match the breed standard to make him a show contender.

A breeder will usually ask right away if you are interested in a family pet or a future champion. This will help her narrow your choices from the litter. A good breeder should guarantee the health of all her pups, regardless of conformation.

Remember, looks aren't

A show-quality Staffy will have different physical attributes than a pet-quality Staffy, but both can be wonderful family companions.

everything! If a liver-colored Staffy pup selects you as his new owner, his disqualifying color won't diminish the joy and love he will bring to your family.

WHERE TO FIND THE STAFFY OF YOUR DREAMS

Dogs come into our lives in different ways. We buy from a variety of sources, we foster rescued dogs, and we adopt from shelters. Sometimes dogs find us, and we become the adoptees. Often, the dogs' backgrounds are nebulous.

When it comes to acquiring a Staffy, however, it's imperative to know what you're getting. A Staffy of questionable origins may have an unpredictable temperament. What is identified as a purebred Staffy may actually be potluck. It's crucial to find a Staffy breeder with integrity. If your generous instincts lead you to rescue an abused or neglected "Staffy mix," understand that health and/or temperament problems may arise down the road. Are you committed to dealing with them, no matter what?

Responsible Staffy ownership requires education, compassion, patience, and material resources. Start the journey right by finding the best way to bring a Staffy into your life.

Breeders

No matter where you decide to purchase your Staffy, it's important that the dog comes from a reputable source. It's no surprise that a breeder's integrity and commitment to the breed must be determined before buying one of her dogs. This is especially important with the Staffy. Because of the negative press and myths surrounding the bully breeds, you want to ensure that you're getting a true Staffy and not a mixture of similar breeds with unknown physical and/or temperament histories. The last thing you want is a dog who displays unexpected aggression while you're attempting to dispel misconceptions about the breed's temperament.

Even if you decide to adopt an adult Staffy, a breeder is the best place to begin your search. She may have an adult who needs a new home, not because there's anything wrong with the dog but because of circumstances. The dog may need more personal attention than a busy breeder can give, or he may not have developed into the show dog the breeder expected.

A reputable breeder will keep a clean kennel, and her dogs will appear happy and well cared for.

Sometimes a purchased puppy is returned years later to the breeder if unforeseen circumstances force the owner to relinquish her pet. Any breeder worth her salt will take such a dog and find him a suitable home rather than see him dropped off at the nearest shelter or advertised "free to a good home" in the newspaper.

Breeders who have numerous dogs who are no longer breeding sometimes offer adults for adoption into suitable homes, and these dogs will thrive in a single- or two-pet family. It's not that the breeder is casually shucking off a dog who is no longer "useful"—even someone with lots of living space and financial resources cannot responsibly care for too many dogs.

Your instincts can go a long way in determining the integrity of a dog breeder. When you visit one, take note if the kennel is clean, the dogs happy and well cared for, and if at least one parent of the litter is on the premises. You will immediately sense what kind of breeder you're dealing with, but you should also look for the following:

- participation in some kind of organized dog activity or sport
- available references from other clients
- the desire to advance the Staffy breed, not to make money
- willingness to reclaim the Staffy you buy if, at any time

during the dog's life, you become unable to keep him for any reason

- provision of a pedigree chart of your Staffy that goes back three generations
- whether the breeder asks you important questions about your home environment, lifestyle, training intentions, diet preferences, security, or anything else that may affect the dog's life
- a genuine love of Staffies and concern for their welfare

Adoption and Rescue

With so many homeless dogs around the world, providing a stable home for one seems a logical and ethical option for anyone desiring a pet. But even this compassionate action has its pros and cons.

First, true Staffies rarely become available for adoption. More often, some sort of Staffy mix is seen at shelters. You may not know of any trauma the dog experienced prior to adoption that can impact future behavior and temperament. A bully breed of unknown lineage and questionable temperament can prove troublesome. If you have the heart and the patience, though, adopting a Staffy or combination thereof is a rewarding gesture. Adopted dogs often seem to sense their good fortune and repay their new owners by being perfectly wonderful pets.

If you want to adopt a purebred Staffy, rescue may be an option. Numerous breed-

If you want an adult Staffy, consider adopting from a rescue or shelter.

specific rescue organizations across the country are eager to find suitable homes for their dogs. These nonprofit organizations rescue dogs of a specific breed from abusive or neglectful situations. Some people who want to disown their dogs, for whatever reason, give them to rescue societies instead of shelters. Occasionally, a dog will be rescued from a nonabusive situation: an elderly owner who died without providing for the dog or an owner who must relocate somewhere that prohibits dogs. In these types of situations, the families don't want to leave the dogs at shelters but have nowhere to place them on their own.

If you can resist the irresistible puppy, adoption of a rescued dog is one of the most charitable decisions you'll ever make.

PAPERWORK

Even in our current paperless society, it seems that everything important in our lives involves paperwork. Staffy ownership is no exception. You receive paperwork from the person or place where you obtain your Staffy, you will maintain records throughout his lifetime, and you will complete paperwork regarding his death and disposition. No matter if you choose to keep all the information on a computer disc or in an actual filing cabinet, you must maintain careful documentation on your Staffy.

Ownership Records

A conscientious breeder or shelter/rescue organization will provide you with a packet of organized information when you take your new puppy home. This should include a sales receipt, basic information on the puppy (birth date, sex, color, etc.), medical history (wormings, first shots), health certificates stating that the parents tested negatively for certain genetic diseases and temperament problems, and any other useful information, such as veterinarian and trainer referrals or toy suggestions. Store everything in one place where you can easily find it when you need it.

Medical Records

Your Staffy's collection of health records starts with a certification from the vet that the puppy is free from infection and contagious diseases. This important document not only gives you peace of mind, it's required if your puppy travels by air to his new home with you. You will also need it later on when you enroll in obedience classes or board your Staffy at a kennel.

Your Staffy puppy should come with a packet of organized information when you bring him home, including a sales receipt, basic information on the puppy, medical history, and health certificates.

The specifics of your Staffy's health data should include the dates of his first distemper, hepatitis, parvovirus, and parainfluenza (DHPP) shot and subsequent vaccinations. He may not have received all his required shots when he goes home with you, depending on his age. Medical documents should indicate exactly which shots are still needed and when.

Health and temperament certifications for both parents should also be included in his overall record. You want to look for Orthopedic Foundation for Animals (OFA) certification that hip dysplasia, a debilitating genetic condition, is not present in his bloodline.

Staffies are known to develop cataracts, so you'll also want to ask the breeder if your new pup's parents were tested for and certified free of eye problems by the Canine Eye Registry Foundation (CERF). These certifications do not guarantee that your Staffy will not develop these or other medical conditions, just that the genes for them are not present in your dog's bloodline.

Registration Papers

If you acquire your Staffy from a reputable breeder, it's likely that the litter has already been registered with the American Kennel Club (AKC). But what does that mean, exactly?

Dog registries, such as the AKC, keep records about dogs. A registry will maintain information like the dog's name, color, sex, and owner, and assign a registration number to this record.

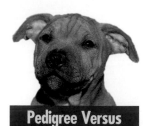

Pedigree Versus Registration

New dog owners are often confused between these two documents. The pedigree is a genealogical record going back at least three generations, including full names and titles of each dog.

The breeder provides an AKC registration application, with her section completed. You must fill in the rest of the information and send it into the AKC with the appropriate fee. They, in turn, will send you a registration certificate declaring your Staffy a "member of the club."

A pedigree and DNA profile are usually included in the records, sometimes known as the dog's "papers." Once you take home the dog, you should advise the registry of the change in ownership. You won't be issued a new certificate, however, and the dog's registered name cannot be changed.

The registered name is usually something long and complex that identifies the breeding kennel, combined with another pertinent name or phrase. Titles may precede and/or follow the name. For example, Ch. Moonstruck the Stamler Express is a Staffy owned by a kennel called Moonstruck Staffords and whose official name is "The Stamler Express." He has earned the conformation title of Champion, indicated as the prefix "Ch." For short, he is called "Stamler." Another example is Yankeestaff Cupid's Arrow CD RN CGC. Known as "Maybelle" to her friends and family, this Staffy was bred at Yankeestaff Kennels and has earned the titles of Companion Dog (CD) in obedience, Rally Novice (RN) in the sport of rally, and Canine Good Citizen (CGC), an independent obedience program.

If you do change the nickname the breeder gave your puppy, don't worry about confusing him. The name he hears regularly over the long term will be the name he responds to.

Pedigree

A dog's pedigree is a chart depicting his ancestors, and it's important for serious show participants who want champions in their bloodline. The pedigree lists individual relatives with their names, coat colors, and reproduction records.

How does a pedigree differ from a registration certificate? The pedigree is your dog's family tree, a genealogical record of his lineage and their history of performance titles earned that gives you an idea of what to expect from your future show-stopper. The registration certificate is an acknowledgment that your dog has met the requirements of and is duly registered with a particular dog club.

Both the pedigree and litter registration certificate should be provided in your new puppy's information package.

Contract

When you buy a Staffy from a respectable source, you'll most likely enter into a contract as part of your sales documents. In addition to such predictable information as the kennel's name and address, purchaser's name and address, and puppy particulars, there should also be a written guarantee that your new Staffy is free of any known genetic faults, and it should stipulate a purchase price refund if the puppy is returned within a specific time frame. Most breeders will gladly allow the puppy to be returned if the new owners decide that their new pet isn't working out. In fact, if a dog owner finds that, for whatever reason during the dog's life, she can no longer keep the dog, a dedicated breeder would rather reclaim guardianship of the dog than see him arbitrarily given away. This important clause benefits all involved. The original purchaser is consoled that the dog will be in good hands, the dog will be happier than if he ended up in a shelter or receiving inappropriate care, and the breeder is satisfied that no dog from her kennel will ever be homeless.

Feeding Instructions

The information packet you receive with your new Staffy pup will include details on what kind of food the breeder feeds, how much, and how often. For first-time puppy owners, this information is a helpful guideline. It also acquaints you with the basics of dog nutrition. Even if you are partial to a certain dog food different from what the breeder has been feeding, it's a good idea to continue with it for a while. Changes in diet can upset a dog's stomach, especially the immature digestive system of a puppy. The breeder should have been feeding a high-quality puppy food, but if you are adamant about using something else, introduce it very gradually into the puppy's diet. Start with one part new food to three parts familiar food for several days. If your Staffy appears to tolerate the change, gradually increase the ratio of new food to familiar food until he is eating only the food you prefer.

Feeding instructions should also encourage you to provide safe chew toys for your puppy, who will need to chew—a lot—while he's teething. He will have no trouble chewing on anything at hand, including your hand! It's crucial that chew toys be virtually indestructible. You don't want a toy or bone that can break off in pieces and potentially choke or injure the puppy. Without appropriate chew toys, a puppy will gnaw on

furniture, door jambs, baseboards, or any number of interesting, challenging objects in your home. Aside from preventing the destruction of your home, you want to prevent your Staffy from ingesting wood splinters, bits of drywall, paint chips, or any other indigestible substance that poses not only a choking hazard but that is toxic or injurious.

GENERAL HOME PREPARATION

Preparing your home for your new Staffy means that you must take the time to puppy proof the house and yard, arrange for the puppy to meet his new family, set up a schedule, and have the proper supplies on hand.

Puppy Proofing Your Home

Once you've set the date to bring home your newest family member, you'll want to ensure that his environment is safe and hospitable. Naturally, your new pup will not be left uncrated and unsupervised, but you still need to identify any potential household hazards. A teething puppy will put anything he finds in his mouth, and you definitely do not want him to discover a delectably chewy electrical cord or the intriguing spray bottle of bathroom cleaner.

Even if you've already thought of everything that may prove dangerous to your new Staffy, perform a walk-through of every area he will be permitted to access, including the house, garage, and yard. Dangers often lurk disguised in unlikely places, including:

- toxic houseplants and yard greenery
- balcony or elevated deck railings that are spaced far enough apart to trap a puppy's questing head or to allow him to fall through completely
- the garage and its host of sharp tools and toxic fluids, especially antifreeze, which tastes sweet but can kill a dog in minutes; a puppy may also decide that the big tires of the family car make cozy nap spots—if someone takes the car out but isn't aware of the puppy's presence…enough said
- heavy objects on shelves that a curious puppy can pull off or topple, injuring or crushing him in the process
- swimming pools, wading pools, hot tubs, and even fish ponds
- small items like thumbtacks, writing instruments, matches, keys, and razors
- toxic ingestibles like alcohol, chocolate, and onions
- pesticides and cleaning agents used routinely around the house
- steep stairs and tall furniture from which a small puppy could fall

Your new dog's adjustment will be much less stressful for you and your family if you take the time to make his new environment a safe, happy place to live.

"Faux Chocolate" Faux Pas

A good dog owner knows never to feed a dog chocolate, but what about artificially flavored chocolate dog treats? They may be safe, but it's not a good idea to foster the dog's taste for a dangerous substance, even a harmless substitute. Chocolate dangers can be insidious. For example, bark mulch can contain cocoa hulls which, if consumed even in small amounts, can kill.

The AKC and Other Registries and Clubs

The American Kennel Club (AKC) is the largest and best-known dog registry in the US, but it is by no means the only one. The United Kennel Club (UKC) was established in 1898 specifically to register the then newly emerging American Pit Bull Terrier (APBT), a breed not recognized by the AKC. The AmStaff and the Staffy, both APBT relatives, are AKC recognized.

The Fédération Cynologique Internationale (FCI) is an international organization that doesn't register dogs but maintains breed standards and related records for national kennel clubs around the world. It operates like the AKC in that it issues pedigree certificates and registers breed clubs.

While certification and registration are important, they are not barometers of your Staffy's capacity for love and companionship. And isn't that really what it's all about?

Meet the "Siblings"

Because of his reputation for compatibility with children, the Staffy is a favorite breed choice for families with kids. It's a good idea to involve the entire family in the puppy acquisition process. Not only is it a chance for the dog to acquaint himself with his new family members, it's a good place to begin teaching the kids about basic puppy behaviors and needs.

In a multi-child family, discourage the kids from crowding around the pup all at once so that he doesn't feel intimidated or overwhelmed. Have the children approach the pup one at a time to give him a chance to familiarize himself with each one.

It's preferable to wait until children are old enough to understand proper treatment and handling of dogs, especially puppies. What a one-year-old child thinks is a gentle pat on the head may actually be an uncoordinated whack on an already stressed puppy in a strange environment. Similarly, a toddler's eager hug can be perceived as a scary strangle-hold. Toddlers and very young children must be taught to gently and slowly interact with the dog.

Puppy proof your home to keep both your new dog and your belongings safe.

If you add a Staffy to the family while the kids are still young, be prepared to supervise interaction at all times. This is for your children's protection as well as for the puppy's. Many dogs, and especially Staffies, have a sense of what children of a certain age can tolerate in the way of typical play, but mouthing is a large part of puppy

behavior. A youngster can receive an accidental nip by those needle-sharp puppy teeth, causing trauma and drama all around.

Generally, children aged six and older are ready to learn the do's and don'ts of pet care and interaction. For their safety and well-being, teach your kids never to:

- Sneak up on a dog to surprise him. A common response to surprise is a bite.
- Disturb a dog who is sleeping or eating. Protective instincts around food can produce a growl or bite.
- Take a toy away from the dog while he's playing with it, or pilfer a dog toy for the child's use. Children's toys should be kept away from the dog and vice versa. Dogs and children should not be in competition for toy ownership.
- Overly roughhouse with a puppy.

Care of the family dog is a great opportunity for parents to teach children about responsibility and compassion. A child entrusted with keeping the Staffy's water bowl filled will enjoy the sense of importance and satisfaction that comes from meeting obligations. Remember to emphasize that your Staffy is a living, feeling creature, not a toy or a novelty soon forgotten. Explain that the family pet needs to feel as safe and loved as the child does. Most children are delighted to provide that kind of care and affection.

Meet the Pets

Adding a Staffy to a multiple-pet household involves its own set of guidelines to foster a successful cohabitation. Remember that the Staffy's deep-seated animal aggression may be lying dormant in his genetic composition. A certain amount of enmity toward other dogs can manifest itself, so it's important to immediately identify any potential personality clashes or dominance issues that can affect family harmony.

Dogs

If possible, choose a dog of the opposite sex from the one you already have. Competition for dominance seems to be worse between two dogs of the same gender, although exceptions exist. If you don't plan to show or breed your Staffies, commit to altering them at an appropriate age. The absence of hormones, especially in males, seems to ameliorate any aggressive tendencies.

Whenever possible, allow the established dog to meet his new buddy a couple of times before the newbie comes home to stay. This will give them a chance to become acquainted, making the new dog less of an interloper. Getting-to-know-you meetings should take place on neutral territory, such as a park, where neither dog feels it necessary to protect his turf. If they show friendly interest in each other with no overt jealousy, they'll likely become bosom buddies. Oh, there will be a squabble here and there at home, usually because the new dog has gotten a little too close to big brother's dinner or is pestering big sister to play when all she wants to do is snooze. These skirmishes usually work themselves out.

When a New Baby Joins the Family

When a new baby comes home, the family dog may get short shrift. Make sure that your Staffy understands that this new human isn't replacing him in your affections. Introduce the baby to your Staffy before coming home from the hospital by letting him sniff a blanket or shirt with the baby's scent on it. When baby arrives, allow your Staffy to sniff her. Pay equal attention to the dog, even when you have company, and give extra treats and toys. It won't be long before the "nanny dog" starts living up to the name!

In general, the Staffy's predisposition for dog aggression may make it difficult for him to live with other dogs, so it's important to evaluate your individual dog and make an informed decision.

Cats

Cat and new dog introductions should be handled tactfully. Cats typically resent intruders and will keep their distance for a few weeks until they realize that the stranger is there to stay. First-time introductions should defer to the cat's seniority among the family's pets. Hold the puppy in your arms, and allow the cat to freely sniff and inspect the new arrival.

Other Pet Types

If you have small pets such as hamsters or rabbits, having an open-house introduction to your new dog is risky. Staffies can have a strong prey drive and might consider your guinea pig to be a toy instead of a playmate. Terriers are meant to hunt and track small animals, and instinct may kick in when face to face with a rodent or other small animal. Keep these pets in their cages, but allow the dog to sniff them through the cage. Dogs raised from puppyhood with other pets in the home usually do quite well, as long as boundaries are established and respected.

Setting Up a Schedule

Virtually everything in your new puppy's life will take place on a timetable. He will eat three or four times a day, sleep every few hours, go outside to eliminate after every nap and meal, and learn to love his crate as a his private suite. Your time will not be your own for a while, but the ultimate joys far outweigh the temporary inconveniences. If adults in the family work full time, plan to take a week or two off when you bring your Staffy puppy home. While he's settling in, you will have erratic sleep and a disrupted routine, so it's best to devote yourself fully to this adjustment phase.

A puppy will usually awake at the crack of dawn, followed by a potty trip outside, then breakfast. He will eat small meals about four times a day as his little stomach continues to mature. This means at least six to seven guaranteed potty trips per day: after every meal, upon waking in the morning, before bedtime, and after every nap. He cannot hold his bladder or bowels for very long, and you will soon learn to read the pup's signals that elimination is imminent, such as circling the floor and sniffing, or a sudden distraction from play. Repetition is the fast track to housetraining, so establish your daily schedule and stick to it. If you absolutely cannot be at home while your new puppy is acclimating to his new environment, secure a friend or professional pet sitter to keep up the feeding and elimination schedule.

Similarly, avoid bringing home a new dog during chaotic holidays or vacations when your routine is disrupted. A puppy's abrupt removal from the familiarity of his dam and littermates is traumatic in itself. Try not to add to the upheaval by bringing him home under hectic conditions.

Supplies

You wouldn't think of bringing home a new baby from the hospital without first stocking up on diapers, formula, nursery furniture, and a million other necessities. Likewise, you shouldn't bring home a new Staffy—puppy or adult—without laying in some all-important supplies. Preparation will help avoid stress and make your Staffy's adjustment easier on both of you.

Bowls

Not surprisingly, the first items to procure for your new Staffy are food and water dishes. These come in a vast

Urban Living

People who live in cities have unique circumstances that require extra attention when adding a dog to the family. Their daily lives include issues that suburbanites rarely need to consider, such as elevators, escalators, rooftops, windows, and balconies. Special thought must be given to a dog's place in the urban scheme of things.

Elevators

In a large apartment building, your Staffy might ride in an elevator several times a day. If he isn't acclimated to it early, he may become frightened by the dinging chimes, noisy doors, and rising and falling sensations. The first few rides for a young puppy should be in the security of your arms. Once he's trained to walk on a leash, put the collar and lead on him for his trips in the elevator, keeping an eagle eye out for missteps in the gap between car and floor. Keep him on a short leash and your hand on the door to prevent it from closing unexpectedly. Allow the pup to enter first, then quickly follow. This prevents the elevator doors from closing with you on the inside and the dog on the outside, separated by the leash. If the car is full of people, you may want to pick up your little guy during the ride so that he isn't accidentally stepped on or crushed. Arm yourself with some paper towels in case of accidental elimination from all the excitement. And if there's another animal passenger already aboard, pass on the ride and wait for the next elevator. Excitement in a confined space could lead to an altercation.

Escalators

Most escalators are found in department stores and office buildings, two places your Staffy probably won't be visiting. However, airports have them, and your dog may be traveling by air sometime. The guidelines for dogs and escalators are straightforward: Never let a leashed dog walk on or off an escalator. The collapsing steps have been known to catch toenails and toes, causing painful and bloody injuries. Opt instead for the regular stairs or an elevator.

Rooftops

Urban dwellers sometimes substitute apartment building rooftops for the wide-open spaces of a backyard as a place for their dogs to romp. Even with vigilant supervision, this is not a good idea. Dogs have limited distance and depth perception, making rooftops dangerous. Protective barriers like railings don't guarantee your Staffy's safety. If you must take your dog on the roof, keep him on a leash and well away from the edge.

Windows and Balconies

In high-rise dwellings, a fall from an open window spells disaster. If you live in such a building and want to get a dog, install window barriers. Many cities require them for the safety of resident children, so your apartment or condo may already have them. The same caution should be taken with balconies and terraces. Widely spaced railings may have openings too small for a child but big enough for a pup to slip through. Better to keep the puppy indoors until he's outgrown the danger of falling through.

Stainless steel food and water dishes are the best choice for your Staffy.

array of styles and materials, the most common of which are plastic, stainless steel, and ceramic. If you find decorative dishes made from a more unusual material, check with the vet to make sure that it's nothing that can sicken your pup. Sometimes food ingredients chemically react to the material of the bowl and can leach toxins.

The type of bowl is your choice, but keep practicality in mind. Ceramics are pretty but can shatter easily. Plastic is indestructible and lightweight, but scratches and cracks in the plastic may harbor bacteria, and puppies can develop skin rashes from an allergy to the plastic material. Stainless steel may not be the most aesthetically pleasing material, but it's your best bet for a dog bowl. If your kitchen appliances are stainless steel, it will fit right into the decor.

Cleaning Supplies

We don't often consider the contents of the utility closet too carefully, but adding a dog to the family means added dirt. Staffies are naturally clean dogs, but they can still track in dirt, have accidents, and become sick. Having the right cleaning supplies on hand will take some of the frustration out of ruined carpets and repeated accidents.

Common sense tells you that if your Staffy's paws are muddy or dirty, use an old towel or rag to wipe them off before he comes inside. You don't need to do a meticulous foot bath, just a quick swipe of a towel, with a pass between the toes and under the toenails to remove the most dirt.

While housetraining a puppy, accidents are a fact of life. Many people prefer to keep their pup in a confined area with a tile or vinyl floor to make cleanup easier, but a little "gift" left on the carpet is bound to happen until your Staffy can control his young bladder and bowels for longer periods of time. In addition to removing and preventing unsightly stains, you also need to neutralize the odor. Dogs naturally seek out odors of urine and feces that identify the location as a good elimination spot. Your Staffy pup will be drawn to the scent on your carpet and eliminate there again. Cleaning and disinfecting products don't neutralize this odor. You'll need to buy a special product designed especially for pet stains and odors to prevent a return to the scene of the crime. Your vet or pet supply store can suggest which ones are effective and nonhazardous to pets, children, and the environment.

Collar and Leash

An appropriately sized collar and leash are must-haves for the new Staffy in the family. You'll want to begin a puppy's leash training early, so the sooner he learns to tolerate a collar, the sooner you can begin. The preferred type is an adjustable nylon buckle collar small enough to fit a puppy's little neck. You may have to upgrade to a larger collar as he grows if the buckle adjustment has limited expansion. A properly fitting collar should not exert undue pressure on the neck yet should be small enough that he can't wriggle his head out of it. Chain collars, if desired, should be used only during training sessions because the links can easily catch on objects and hurt or choke the puppy.

Your Staffy's leash should be about 5 to 6 feet (1.5 to 2 m) long and of a strong, flexible fabric such as nylon or leather. Retractable leashes are not ideal for adult Staffies, who are strong enough to snap the slender cord right out of the plastic housing. Your local pet supply store can help you choose the right collar and leash for your Staffy.

Grooming Supplies

The Staffy is a low-maintenance breed when it comes to grooming. The short, sleek coat of a healthy Staffy needs only minimal care to keep it looking gorgeous. A soft brush or grooming glove is all you need to remove

Handy Clean-Up Supplies

- moist baby wipes or doggy wipes for muddy paws, etc.
- odor neutralizer and stain remover
- paper towels for blotting carpet accidents
- gentle, nontoxic, all-purpose cleaning spray for cleaning up soiled floors

An adjustable nylon buckle collar is a good choice for your Staffy puppy's little neck.

loose hairs and dander from his fur. Later on, when he's matured, you may want to buy a special shedding comb for those semi-annual coat-blowing sheddings.

The Staffy's grooming cabinet should also include a pair of toenail clippers, a soft toothbrush or special textured finger sheath for dental hygiene, cotton balls for ear and eye cleanings, and a mild dog shampoo for the rare times when you need to bathe him. Never use human shampoo, which contains detergents that are too harsh for a dog's skin. Frequent bathing is not only unnecessary for a Staffy, it is discouraged. Too many baths and/or too strong a shampoo will strip the dog's skin of the natural oils that keep his fur shiny and water repellant, and his skin comfortably moisturized. A dull or dandruffy coat, combined with frequent scratching, could indicate a skin issue. Protect your Staffy's skin by bathing him only if he's gotten into something really nasty.

Identification

Even if you're the most conscientious dog owner in the world who can't imagine any circumstances in which your Staffy could become lost, identification is a must. Unfortunately, dogs are sometimes stolen from their own yards; Staffies are particularly desirable to thieves looking for fighting "practice" dogs. Stolen and stray dogs are also sold to scientific research facilities. This probably won't happen, but it pays to be prepared. If you don't want to risk losing your Staffy, consider one of the following methods of identifying your dog and improving his chances of returning home.

TAGS

Since you've checked for any breed-specific legislation that may have precluded Staffy ownership, you've probably already learned what kind of dog registration is required in your area. Dog licensing varies from state to state and county to county, so be sure of your local government's requirements. Usually, dog registration includes a numbered tag affixed to your pet's collar. It's also a good idea to have a separate tag made with your name and phone number on it. These tags are inexpensive and easy to get by mail order or at a pet supply store. Be sure to comply with all dog registration requirements so that animal control officials never have a reason to apprehend your Staffy.

Another important tag for your Staffy's collar is the vet-issued proof of rabies vaccination. In the unlikely case that your Staffy bites someone, the first question will be if his vaccinations are up to date. Without ready proof of rabies immunization, officials can order your dog destroyed to test for rabies. Be sure to affix the new rabies tag to your Staffy's collar each time the vaccine is updated.

MICROCHIPPING

Microchipping is a permanent, safe, painless way to ID your Staffy. The microchip is actually a tiny capsule, about the size of a long grain of rice, injected under a flap of skin on the nape of the dog's neck. Inside the capsule is an even tinier chip with a unique number that's been registered with an international registry. Lost dogs who are turned into shelters or animal hospitals are scanned for this microchip. A handheld scanner reads this number, and authorities call it into the registry for a match with the dog's rightful owners. Scientific research facilities also scan dogs brought in as research subjects in case they were stolen or lost.

Microchipping can never be altered, making it an extremely reliable means of identification. The chip itself is made of hypoallergenic material and should not cause your Staffy any discomfort.

Your Staffy needs some type of identification so that he can be returned to you should he ever become lost.

Your Staffy needs some type of identification so that he can be returned to you should he ever become lost.

TATTOOING

Developed by the founders of the National Dog Registry (NDR), tattooing is a simple, affordable way to identify your dog. Unlike human tattoos, pet tattooing is painless. A dog's skin structure is so different from ours that the tattoo pen doesn't need to be inserted very far into the skin's outer surface. Although he may not like the noise of the equipment and body restraint necessary during the procedure, the dog doesn't experience any pain.

Like the microchip, the number tattooed on a dog is registered to a database for matching in the event of a loss. Unlike the microchip, the tattoo is visible to the naked eye and doesn't require any special equipment to read it. The best location for a tattoo is on the inside of the thigh, where hair is sparse and the number can be readily seen, but if the dog is found by someone who is unaware of tattooed identification, the tattoo may go unnoticed. Ink fades over time, so tattoos should be periodically touched up for clarity.

Outerwear

We've all seen those oh-so-precious little outfits adorning chagrined Chihuahuas and Yorkies: ballerinas, leprechauns, even Elvis. Beyond the novelty of dog costumes, however, there is a need for clothing with a purpose.

COLD WEATHER CLOTHES

Although a hardy dog by nature, the Staffy's short, close-lying fur doesn't offer much protection against extreme cold. The breed's energy level is usually high enough to keep them warm for relatively brief outings in cold weather, but there may be times when outerwear is in order.

In addition to making a fashion statement, a dog sweater will help keep your Staffy warm in very windy or freezing conditions. Smaller-size sweaters seem to be more prevalent in stores than larger ones, so you may need to do some hunting for a Staffy-size sweater. Know any knitters? Ask her to make you one!

If you live in the far northern climates or need to be outside in snowy weather, you may want to investigate dog parkas. These outer garments are made of water-repellant material and have the quilted look of down jackets and a snug cloth lining. Some even come with a hood that folds neatly away in a zippered compartment when not in use.

FOOTWEAR

Don't overlook your Staffy's feet when protecting him from cold weather. He doesn't have the plentiful fur between his toes like the Siberian Husky and the American Eskimo Dog do. Although it's unlikely that a Staffy would be outdoors for any length of time in dangerously cold, wet conditions, his feet can become frostbitten if he is. Dog booties take care of this problem, as well as protect his paws from ice shards that can cut his feet.

Booties are readily available because many show dogs wear them prior to conformation competitions to

How to Measure Your Staffy's Paws

To measure your dog's paws for the right-size booties:

1. Stand him on a blank piece of paper. With a pencil, trace the outline of his paw, including toenails. Be sure that the dog's full weight is on his paws, and keep the pencil tightly against his foot.

2. Measure the length of the outline from heel to tip of toenails. Match the number with the vendor's listed boot sizes.

3. If your dog's feet measure in between sizes, go for the snugger fit so that the boots won't slip off.

Make sure that any toy you buy is appropriately sized for your Staffy.

shield their pristine pedicures. A pet supply store can help you measure your Staffy's feet to get the right size boot.

Similarly, Staffies who must go outside in heavy rain should wear rain-repellant or waterproof jackets. These garments don't always offer much in the way of warmth but they help keep the dog dry. Staffies become chilled easily, and body heat is lost even faster when wet. If he must go outside in a chilly autumn downpour, a raincoat may not be a bad idea.

Toys

Providing your Staffy with safe, appropriate toys is not indulgent—it's necessary. An unoccupied, unexercised Staffy will look for any available outlet for his pent-up energy, resulting in property destruction and potential danger to your dog. It's your responsibility as a Staffy owner to provide him with mentally stimulating and physically exerting playthings.

Dog toys don't have to be fancy or expensive. A simple tennis ball provides lots of fetching fun and is a good opportunity for you two to play together. Even soccer-sized balls make good toys to chase around the yard. Sturdy twists of rope are popular toys that are safe for a dog's gums and teeth, and sturdy chew toys provide good workouts for his teeth and gums and also satisfy the urge to chew.

Toys to avoid include stuffed animals with button-like features that can be ripped off or squeaky toys that are easily torn apart. Some also advise that you shun squeaky toys that resemble actual objects you don't want your dog to chew, like shoes.

Be sure that any toy you buy is appropriately sized

A Staffy needs safe, appropriate toys to help him expend energy and alleviate boredom.

for your Staffy. When he's a puppy, small chew toys are fine, but once he's reached his full growth, small or slender chew toys become choking hazards. Likewise for small or flimsy balls. As your Staffy grows, replace potentially hazardous puppy toys with larger, sturdier ones—Nylabone makes some good ones.

What kind of toy can occupy an intelligent adult Staffy? This is where creativity comes in. Nowadays you can purchase toys specifically designed to engage a dog's mind. This includes hollow balls with openings that dispense treats. Even a large, hollow chew toy stuffed with a tablespoon of peanut butter will keep him busy for a while. A flying disc is another toy that combines entertainment with exercise. (Buy a "floppy disc" because a hard plastic one can chip teeth or cause minor injury.)

It's obvious that adding a Staffy to the family is no flight of fancy. But for all the time and money invested in preparation and care, you will be rewarded a hundredfold with a loving and loyal pet.

4

FEEDING

Your Staffordshire Bull Terrier

When humans domesticated the dog, they eliminated the wild animal's need to spend the better part of each day in search of food. Now it falls to us to make sure that our companion animals' nutritional needs are met. This means understanding that a dog's physiology requires a diet different from that of humans and that fulfilling those dietary needs may take some effort. Without proper nutrition, a Staffy pup will not grow into the strong, vigorous dog he's destined to be. His mental development also may suffer. Staffy ownership includes familiarizing yourself with the dietary options available for dogs before selecting the one that best suits your Staffy's needs.

FOOD BASICS

Good nutrition does more than contribute to a dog's overall well-being. It prevents dietary deficiency diseases and helps fend off infections by keeping his immune system working at full throttle. A wholesome dog food should contain the proper amounts of carbohydrates, fats, minerals, proteins, and vitamins, which all work together to keep your Staffy looking and feeling his best. He also needs the proper amount of water in his diet. The greater your understanding of canine nutrition, the easier it will be to select the diet that is right for him.

Carbohydrates

Carbohydrates comprise sugars, starch, and cellulose. Because meat doesn't naturally provide enough carbohydrates for a dog's well-rounded diet, he must get it from plant-based sources. In the wild, this means whatever plant matter is in his prey's stomach. In our homes, this means healthy sources like boiled potatoes, carrots, rice, and whole grains.

Carbohydrates aid digestion and elimination in much the same way that high-fiber diets help humans. Approximately 5 percent of a Staffy's complete diet should be fiber from carbohydrates. Excess carbs are stored in the body for later use, but it's doubtful a healthy, active Staffy would ever have an excess!

A wholesome, nutritious diet will help your dog look and feel his best.

Fats

Fats are used as an energy source, and they keep your Staffy's skin healthy and his coat shiny. Finding the right balance of fats is important. A diet too rich in fats leads to unhealthy weight gain, which can bring on further health problems. Insufficient fats in the diet can cause itchy skin, a dull coat, dandruff, and sometimes ear infections; a deficiency also can make your Staffy overly sensitive to cold.

The energetic Staffy relies on fats as a ready energy source. They also enhance the taste of his food, encouraging healthy eating habits. If you feel that your Staffy's diet could use a boost in healthy fats, ask your vet about a fat supplement that's right for your dog.

Types of Dog Bowls

Choosing food and water bowls is a matter of preference, but consider these pros and cons when making your decision:

- Plastic is inexpensive but can become scratched, chewed, stained, and difficult to clean properly. Cracks and scratches in the plastic also can harbor bacteria. Some dogs are allergic to the plastic and develop skin rashes or lesions.

- Stainless steel is more sanitary than plastic but so lightweight that the bowl can easily be knocked over.

- Ceramic dishes are both stable and sanitary but easily chipped and broken. The glazes they're made with may have chemical reactions to certain foods and leach toxins into the food. If you just have to have a decorative ceramic dog dish, find out exactly what materials it's made of. Check with your vet about any potential digestive issues.

Minerals

Minerals are nutrients that come from the earth and water.

- **Calcium and phosphorus:** Work together to prevent rickets and other bone deformities. They also aid in tooth formation, muscle development, and lactation in nursing bitches.
- **Cobalt (with manganese):** Aids normal growth and a healthy reproductive system.
- **Iodine:** Prevents goiter or enlarged thyroid.
- **Iron (with copper):** Required for healthy blood.
- **Magnesium:** Helps synthesize proteins and prevents convulsions and nervous system disorders.
- **Potassium:** Aids normal growth and keeps nerves and muscles healthy.
- **Sodium and chlorine:** Maintain appetite and a normal activity level.
- **Zinc:** Promotes healthy skin.

Minerals can be easily oversupplemented, so check with your veterinarian first.

Proteins

Protein is important for bone growth, tissue healing, and daily replacement of spent body tissues. All animal tissue has a relatively high level of protein, but it is not stored in the body. Therefore, your Staffy must obtain a fresh supply from his food every day. Dogs are primarily carnivorous, so most of the digestible protein they need comes from meat. Certain plants, such as legumes, also can provide dietary protein. When a wild carnivore kills and eats prey, he consumes the entire animal, including the stomach and its contents. Most prey animals are herbivores, thereby

Fats keep a dog's skin healthy and his coat shiny.

Proteins are important for bone growth and tissue healing.

providing the carnivore with the required amount of dietary plant matter. Isn't nature clever?

Humans are not always as clever. We may be encouraged to eat our vegetables, but if we feed our dogs too much indigestible vegetable protein, colic and/or diarrhea can result.

Proteins comprise about 25 "building blocks" called amino acids. Ten of these are "essential," meaning they cannot be manufactured in the body and must be obtained from food. That leaves 15 nonessential amino acids that are produced within the body.

A healthy diet includes plenty of lean protein.

Vitamins

A balanced diet should provide all the vitamins your Staffy needs. Supplementation should only be with your vet's approval. It's easy to overdose supplements and create health issues that didn't exist before. To provide the necessary vitamins in your dog's diet, it's important to know what each one does.

- **Vitamin A:** Vitamin A is used for fat absorption, keeping your Staffy's coat glossy. It also promotes good eyesight, normal growth rate, and reproduction.
- **B Vitamins:** These vitamins promote healthy skin, coat, skin, appetite, growth, and eyes. They also protect the nervous system and aid metabolism.
- **Vitamin C:** This vitamin is synthesized in a dog's liver, so it's not typically listed in commercial dog food analyses.
- **Vitamin D:** Vitamin D is essential for healthy bones, teeth, and good muscle tone, but it must be taken with the proper ratio of calcium and phosphorus, typically found in the prey animal's bones and ligaments.
- **Vitamin E:** This vitamin is required for proper muscle function, internal and reproductive organs, and all cell

Your Staffy should always have clean, cool water available.

membrane function. Check the package of your dog's food for vitamin information.

- **Vitamin K:** Like vitamin C, vitamin K is not typically listed in commercial dog food analyses. It is synthesized in the digestive tract.

Water

The average dog's body consists of about two-thirds water, so it's no surprise that water is necessary for survival. Dogs don't perspire the same way humans do, but they do lose water through sweat glands in their feet, by panting, and via the kidneys. As a guideline for daily water consumption, a healthy dog should consume (from food and drink) 1/2 to 3/4 fluid ounces (15 to 22 ml) per 1 pound (0.5 kg) of body weight. In hot weather or strenuous exercise, he'll need more. Make sure that your Staffy always has clean, cool water available. Excessive drinking can be a symptom of illness, so talk to your veterinarian if you notice your Staffy drinking more than usual.

THE DO'S AND DON'TS OF DOG FEEDING

Sometimes the food that's best for your dog is not always the handiest or cheapest, but your commitment to your Staffy's care different dietary needs, which means we can easily purchase food formulated especially for puppies, active adults, overweight dogs, and senior citizens. Whichever type of commercial food you choose, make sure that it's a well-balanced, high-quality brand that meets your dog's nutritional needs.

Although commercial dog food is very convenient, there are still choices to be made within this food type.

Dry Food (Kibble)

A popular and economical food choice, dry dog food keeps well without refrigeration and may be bought in bulk quantities. The chewing action of the crunchy food also helps reduce tartar buildup on your dog's teeth. Read package labels carefully to determine food quality. Choose a brand that lists a wholesome digestible protein, such as chicken or lamb, as a primary ingredient (one of the first four listed).

Dry food, or kibble, is a popular and economical food choice.

Canned (Wet) Food

Canned food smells and tastes great to a dog, and its long shelf life makes it easy to purchase and convenient to store. But it can be costly, and the soft consistency does little for your Staffy's oral hygiene. It is readily available at supermarkets and larger convenience stores, but how much digestible protein does it really provide? How much of the food is filler (processed grain, grain hulls, and/or animal by-products)? Read the labels to find a brand that offers the most nutrition.

Semi-Moist Food

These are the foods shaped like chops, burgers, or other meaty-looking tidbits meant to lure consumers with the insinuation that their dog will be eating an equivalent to prime rib or a nice T-bone. But these foods are usually the least wholesome of all commercial dog foods, filled with artificial colors, flavors, and aromas. They don't serve well as an exclusive diet, but they can be tasty occasional treats. Let's face it: Your Staffy doesn't understand what the meat shapes mean, anyway!

Noncommercial Foods

Noncommercial dog foods are not easily found in supermarkets or convenience stores, but they are popular enough that a little research should turn up a source, such as a butcher shop or meat purveyor, in your general area. You might ask around if there's a raw-food buying coop, where a group of dog owners share the expense of bulk-ordering raw dog food. Meat for pets is often sold at much lower prices than the meat you buy for your dinner table and is of comparable quality. Dogs will also eat animal parts that most humans find distasteful, so they are very inexpensive. Talk to your breeder, vet, or other dog owners about local sources for noncommercial foods.

The Home-Cooked Diet

Instead of leaving their Staffies' nutrition in the hands of others, some owners prefer to be in complete control of their dogs' nutrition. When properly researched and prepared, a homemade diet is an excellent way to ensure that your Staffy is eating right.

It's important to understand that the home-cooked diet is not a simple matter of opening a can or tearing open a pouch. It requires considerable education and experience to be sure that you're giving your Staffy the nutrients he needs. Preparation is time consuming and more expensive than buying commercially prepared dog food. In fact, the numbers of people who feed only home-cooked food to their

Storing Dog Food

Dry dog food should be stored in an airtight container to maintain freshness and discourage bugs or rodents. Commercial dog foods usually have some type of preservative added to extend shelf life, but check the expiration date on the side of the bag. Don't buy or serve dog food with an expired date.

Canned or wet leftover dog food should be tightly covered and stored in the refrigerator. The next time you serve it, you can take the chill off by putting it in the microwave for a few seconds beforehand.

Semi-moist dog foods are usually packaged in individual servings, eliminating leftovers. Store unopened packets where your Staffy can't access them. If you're using the semi-moist morsels as treats, transfer them to a self-closing plastic bag or airtight container so that they don't dry out.

treats you give your Staffy as it is to know the quality of his food. "Junk food" snacks and unwholesome treats can negate all the health benefits you've worked hard to provide in his diet. As with commercial dog food, commercially sold treats come in a wide variety of shapes, sizes, flavors, and compositions. Some are made with only natural, healthy ingredients suitable for human consumption; others contain mostly chemicals and animal by-products. The former tend to be found in specialty pet supply stores, while the latter tend to be on supermarket shelves. Fortunately, the whole- and natural-food supermarkets that are springing up everywhere usually include a pet products aisle where you can find nutritious dog treats. The treats may cost a little more, but the ingredients are top quality.

You may not realize it, but some of the best dog treats are right in your own kitchen. Share some sliced apple or bell pepper with your Staffy. Plain rice cakes are a satisfying, crunchy snack, as is a handful of whole-grain cereal. Spread on a tablespoonful of natural peanut butter, and you'll have one happy Staffy. Remember, though, that many "people foods" can make a dog very sick, so check with your vet before experimenting.

Chew Bones

The primal need to chew is alive and well in our dogs, and bones are the logical choice to satisfy that urge. If your Staffy is eating a BARF (Biologically Appropriate Raw Food) diet, he is probably consuming the small poultry bones that are nutritious and satisfyingly crunchy, but it's not the same as gnawing on a large marrow bone.

It bears repeating that cooked bones can splinter easily and cause internal injury or choking. For your Staffy's chewing pleasure and his safety, go with large soup bones sold in the meat section of your supermarket or knuckle bones sold at pet supply stores. The thick bone will give his teeth and gums a good workout, and he'll enjoy eating the marrow inside. Over time, though, your Staffy may succeed in breaking off small shards of bone. These pieces can lacerate the soft tissues of his

Artificial bones made of strong, hard material make good chew toys.

mouth and pose a choking hazard. When the bone becomes too brittle, replace it.

Artificial bones made of strong, hard material, like Nylabones, make good chew toys. Some are coated with a tasty meat or peanut butter flavor; others have a nubby texture designed to massage the dog's gums as he chews or mint flavor to freshen his breath. These "bones" are very durable and convenient to find.

Supplements

Although a healthy diet should provide all the nutrients your Staffy needs, there may be times in a dog's life when supplements are beneficial. A pregnant or nursing female needs a little more food than she normally does. Show dogs who travel frequently may experience more stress than homebodies and so need more nutrition. A malnourished dog rescued from an abusive home will need careful reintroduction to regular meals. If you think that your Staffy's diet should be supplemented, consult your vet first. As mentioned earlier, supplements are easily overdosed, which can lead to a variety of ailments.

FEEDING SCHEDULES

There are basically two ways to feed your Staffy: free feeding and scheduled feeding. As the name implies, free feeding means that unlimited food is available at all times. Scheduled feeding means eating finite amounts at designated times, the healthiest way to feed a Staffy. To see why scheduled feeding is best for your Staffy, you'll need to understand the options and their repercussions.

Scheduled Feeding

Just like human babies, Staffy puppies will eat frequent, small meals in between naps and playtime, amounting to four times a day. How much they eat varies with each dog, but pups should have about 1/4 cup (59 ml) of food at each meal. Meal size will grow as the puppy grows, and the frequency will diminish. Commercial dog foods for puppies have recommended feeding amounts and schedules listed on the package, or you can consult with your vet or breeder.

To keep the "scheduled" in scheduled feeding, limit the time that meals are available. Picky eaters are not allowed! Even if your Staffy pup doesn't finish his meal immediately, take the dish away after about ten minutes. He'll quickly learn that he has a certain window of opportunity to eat, or he'll have to bide the time until his next meal.

Scheduled feedings also help regulate elimination, which in turn reinforces your housetraining. Take him outside immediately after every meal, and praise him when he does his business.

Free Feeding

Imagine having a smorgasbord available to you at home, around the clock, every day of the week. That's what free feeding your Staffy would be. Most dogs won't stop eating when they no longer feel hungry; they'll keep eating if it tastes good or if they feel competition with other pets for food. A free-fed Staffy will probably become overweight, lethargic, and less interested in food, which can impede obedience training. It's hard to get excited about food when it's there for the taking all the time.

Free feeding can promote begging, an annoying habit you don't want to foster. The food in your Staffy's "buffet"

will soon bore him, and your dinner will smell a lot more tempting. It won't be long before he ignores his food altogether and waits for handouts from your dinner table. This is not only ill-mannered behavior, but it deprives him of the specific nutrition his own food provides.

Free feeding also deprives you of an important tool in judging your Staffy's health. A dog's appetite and eating habits are barometers for his well-being. One of the first inklings you may have that your dog isn't feeling well is a lack of appetite. A decreased interest in food at regular mealtimes may indicate a health issue. But if a dog has food available all day long, how would you be able to differentiate an atypical loss of appetite from a temporary disinterest in food?

A dog's digestive system is not designed to accommodate continuous eating. Dogs in the wild have long interludes between meals, giving their bodies a chance to digest and prepare for the next feeding. The key to a healthy, happy dog is to allow his body to function as nature intended.

FEEDING FOR ALL LIFE STAGES

Just as with humans, dogs have different nutritional needs at different times in their lives. You may feed your Staffy pup a commercial food formula that he won't need when he becomes an adult. Similarly, an elderly dog may have digestive or dental issues that require a special diet to accommodate his changing physiology. Part of a dog owner's education is to understand the nutritional needs of all life stages.

Feeding Your Staffy Puppy

Puppy nutrition is pretty much the same across the board, regardless of breed. Puppies need frequent, small meals of high-quality food and fresh water available at all times. Your puppy will have been weaned at about four to six weeks of age, so find out what solid food the breeder has been giving the litter. Even if you want to ultimately switch to a different brand or type, you should continue with the food he's used to and gradually make the change by mixing in the new food in increasing proportions. His developing digestive system isn't able to handle abrupt dietary changes.

As a general rule of thumb, a Staffy pup will eat four times a day until he's about two years old. As he matures, the number of feedings can be reduced to three, then to two as he reaches adulthood. Dogs mature at individual rates, so be flexible.

How much food should your Staffy pup consume at each meal? Your breeder or vet can guide you on this, and commercial dog food packages usually provide charts to help you. Puppies can have voracious appetites, however, so be careful not to overfeed. If you feel that your Staffy is insatiable and your vet approves, add a little cooked rice or whole-grain, low-sugar breakfast cereal to his puppy food at mealtime. It won't add a lot of extra calories, and the fiber will keep him satisfied longer.

Make sure that your Staffy puppy's treats are made of wholesome, easily digested ingredients.

Treats will certainly be a part of your Staffy pup's diet, especially once you start obedience training and housetraining. Appropriate puppy treats can be store bought or homemade; either way, make sure that they are made of wholesome, easily digested ingredients. And remember that treats supplement your Staffy's diet, not replace his primary food.

Feeding Your Adult Staffy

Generally speaking, a dog is considered fully grown after the age of two years, although some will say that an 18-month-old is on the cusp of adulthood. Some dogs mature faster than others. A typical adult Staffy eats twice a day, with his total daily allotment of food divided into the two meals. This can vary, of course, depending on your dog's individual needs. An altered adult will require less food than an active show dog. A Staffy who participates in demanding dog sports will require more food than a dog on the conformation circuit. Even dogs with equivalent lifestyles can have different metabolisms that call for more or less food. Weather has an impact, too; some dogs will eat more in winter than in summer. As your Staffy grows, you will come to gauge what he needs and when he needs it. The proof is in his bright eyes, shiny coat, well-developed musculature, and happy disposition.

One or Two Meals per Day?

An old-fashioned school of thought says that adult dogs should eat a single meal per day, but a healthier choice is to divide his daily ration into two meals. Not only will this more efficiently fuel his body, he'll be less likely to wolf down his food, which can cause minor stomach upsets like gas and indigestion or the dangerous condition of gastric torsion, sometimes known as "bloat."

Feeding the Senior Staffy

As with humans, a dog's metabolism slows down with age. Here again, the actual aging rate can vary from dog to dog, so there's no magic number that automatically brands a Staffy as a senior citizen. From about the age of eight years, you may begin to notice changes in your Staffy. He may tire more quickly than he used to and sleep more. His fur may start to show some gray. And just like us, the older Staffy may develop physical problems like arthritis and dental problems.

If your senior Staffy starts to exhibit less interest in his food, a dental issue may be the cause. If he has painful teeth or gums, mealtime can be unpleasant for him. Have his mouth checked by the vet, who can suggest ways to work around the problem, such as feeding softer foods. Your Staffy's senses may become duller with age, meaning his food will smell and taste less appetizing to him. If he becomes a picky eater, you can try warming his food to give it a more tantalizing aroma or separating it into smaller meals offered several times a day. Sometimes a change in routine will entice a fussy eater to pay more attention to his food.

Staffies in the geriatric set will thrive on a lower percentage of protein than what they ate during their prime. Commercial dog foods for "seniors" are manufactured with this in mind.

Senior formulas also contain less fat and added nutrients like glucosamine and chondroitin to regenerate cartilage growth in the joints. A comparison of food package labels will spell out the differences.

OBESITY

An overweight dog is an unhealthy dog. Obesity puts added stress on the joints and forces a dog's internal organs to work harder. Don't make the mistake of equating food with love. It's okay to say no to those entreating eyes when you open the pantry door. Too many treats and too much food at mealtimes may make your Staffy's tail wag, but they will also make his waistline expand. You will show greater love for your dog by keeping his weight at a healthy level.

Dog food packages list recommended servings based on a dog's age and weight. Healthy adult male Staffies typically weigh 28 to 38 pounds (13 to 17 kg), and healthy adult females weigh 24 to 34 pounds (11 to 15 kg). Even a fit Staffy can mask a little extra weight behind his naturally stocky build, so keep your eye on his metabolism and physique as he ages. You will

A nutritious diet, combined with the right amount of exercise, will help keep your Staffy from becoming overweight.

have to reduce the number of calories he ingests according to how much his metabolism slows. This doesn't mean you should deprive him of regular meals—he still needs a certain amount of nutrition to stay healthy, and cutting out meals as a way of putting your Staffy on a diet is not a good idea. Instead, consult

Canine Obesity Concerns

Allowing your Staffy to become obese not only compromises his good looks, but it compromises his good health. Some of the conditions associated with canine obesity are:

- depression
- diabetes
- gastrointestinal disorders
- heart problems
- heat intolerance
- joint and bone problems
- liver disease
- respiratory disease
- skin conditions

your vet, consider a lower-fat, lower-calorie food for senior or overweight dogs, and increase his daily exercise, health permitting. Stock up on low-calorie treats like rice cakes. Take his mind off food with something else to occupy his brain, like a challenging new toy or outdoor game. Keeping your Staffy fit, trim, and happy is one of the best gifts you can give him.

Is Your Staffy Overweight?

The best guideline for judging if your Staffy is losing his figure is his general appearance. He should have a defined "waistline" that begins after the rib cage and tapers toward the haunches. Look up pictures of healthy Staffies of different sizes and corresponding weights. Does yours look like one of these, or is he chunkier?

Regular veterinary checkups are always a good way to learn if your dog is at a proper weight. The first thing they'll do is put your Staffy on the scale. The vet or technician can tell you if he is on the right track.

Another means of gauging proper weight is to run your hand gently over the rib cage. At a proper weight, you should be able to feel your dog's ribs with gentle pressure. If the dog is overweight, you won't readily feel his ribs. If he's underweight, his rib cage will show prominently all the time.

Your Staffy needs the right food for growth, work, and play. You contracted to provide this basic need when you became a dog owner. Live up to your end of the bargain, and your thriving Staffy will repay you many times over.

GROOMING

Your Staffordshire Bull Terrier

The elegant Staffy's handsome appearance carries the added benefit of requiring very little in the way of grooming. His short, sleek coat needs only regular brushing to keep it looking its shiny best. Odor is not usually a problem for the Staffy unless he's met up with a skunk or rolled in something irresistible to him—but stinky to you—like deer or raccoon droppings. Regular bathing should not be necessary to keep the naturally clean Staffy smelling sweet unless he works as a therapy dog. (Some facilities that utilize therapy dogs require them to be bathed before every visit.)

Your Staffy may not need extensive grooming, but you can make regular grooming your special time to bond with each other. Accessories like grooming gloves essentially act the same as petting, so while you're removing loose, dead hair, your Staffy thinks he's getting a massage. You both will enjoy the relaxing contact.

GROOMING AS A HEALTH CHECK

If you need an excuse for daily grooming and bonding with your Staffy, consider it as health care maintenance.

Parasite Problems

A thorough going-over of your dog's skin will alert you to any parasite problems. You can easily detect ticks by running your hand over his smooth coat. A burrowing tick will feel like a disruption in the otherwise smooth "landscape" of his skin, prompting you to take a closer look. Most dog ticks will appear as little brown scabs sticking out of the skin. Deer ticks, however, are so tiny that they are hard to spot. But they can carry Lyme disease, so close inspection of your Staffy's skin is a wise idea. Part your Staffy's short hair with your fingers to examine the skin surface. Deer ticks will look like poppy seeds, but don't let their size fool you. Lyme disease is a serious medical condition that can prove lethal if untreated, so take no chances.

You can also check for fleas while you're grooming your Staffy. Flea "dirt," or excrement, will appear on a dog's skin like specks of ground black pepper. A flea

The Staffy's short, sleek coat needs only regular brushing to keep it looking its best.

infestation is usually accompanied by a lot of scratching, so you'll have good cause to check for fleas if your Staffy is scratching more than usual.

Skin Problems

Even if parasites are not a problem, regular skin checks are useful to make sure that your Staffy isn't suffering from any rashes or other dermatological issues. Keep an eye out for "hot spots," areas of potential irritation that make your Staffy want to lick, scratch, or nip at his skin. White-coated dogs, in particular, seem to experience more skin ailments than darker-coated dogs. A skin check will show up any bumps or lesions that may indicate an allergy or infection.

Dry or dandruffy skin can be annoying and uncomfortable for your Staffy, dulling his otherwise beautiful coat. Many dogs suffer dry skin during the winter months, when dry, warm air heats the home and robs the skin of moisture. Dry skin is easily treated at home by adding 1 tablespoon of canola, safflower, or flaxseed oil to his food. The short-chain fatty acids in these oils lubricate the skin from the inside out. You can also buy oil gelcaps formulated to do the same thing. Your vet will instruct you on the proper dosage for these capsules, which are usually added to your dog's food.

Regular brushing is helpful to dry

Grooming Time = Bonding Time

Grooming is a great way to spend quality time with your Staffy. Because he only needs regular brushing to spruce up, he can relax and enjoy the attention while you remove any dirt from his coat and check for parasites. Use a grooming glove to turn the session into a soothing massage.

skin because it distributes the natural oils secreted from the skin to lubricate it. A persistent skin irritation warrants a visit to the vet because the problem may be more than a temporary or seasonal issue.

GROOMING SUPPLIES

The low-maintenance Staffy requires only a minimum of grooming supplies. A few basics from the pet supply store, and you're all set to keep your dog looking gorgeous.

Brush

The type of brush used most often for Staffies has a handle and medium-soft bristles that make his coat gleam without being too harsh on his skin. A curry brush also comes in handy; it has no handle to grasp but fits into the palm of your hand, with a strap over your knuckles. Usually made of rubber, the curry brush has little nubs all over the grooming surface that massage the skin as well as comb through the hair. This type of brush comes in handy if your Staffy has gotten into something really messy. The nubs remove the worst of the dirt once it has dried.

Comb

The Staffy's short hair doesn't need the meticulous combing of, say, a Yorkshire Terrier or Afghan Hound. However, during

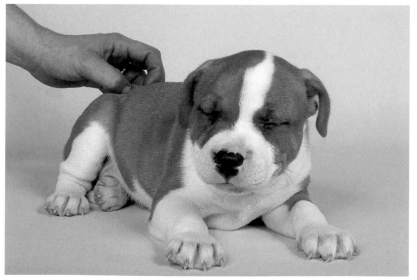

Grooming time provides a great opportunity for you to bond with your dog.

85

shedding times it can be useful to separate the undercoat and remove loose, dead hairs. A shedding comb is effective for this and available at any store that carries pet supplies. The comb has two edges: fine-toothed for areas where the hair is sparse and wide-toothed for more thickly furred areas. The teeth on both edges should have rounded tips to prevent lacerations.

The shedding comb blade typically folds over into a loop, with both ends fitting into the handle, but it can also be used as a straight edge. A gentle pressure as you comb will collect loose hair and feel pleasant to your Staffy. Be extra gentle on sensitive areas.

Toenail clippers are an essential grooming tool.

Nail Clippers

Before dogs were domesticated, their daily treks in search of food kept their toenails trimmed to a serviceable length. When we took over the care and feeding of dogs, it fell to us to take over where nature left off. Staffies who are walked regularly and extensively on hard surfaces don't usually need their nails trimmed, but others need a little help from their human friends. Toenail clippers are essential—they're probably the grooming tool you will use most often.

Nail clippers come in two basic types. The guillotine type, as the name implies, works like a guillotine to sever the nail tip. It works well for puppies whose nails are relatively small and thin. As a dog grows older, his nails will thicken and become harder to cut. That's when the shears-type clippers become necessary. These work in a scissors action to cut the nail.

Many Staffy owners, especially those who participate in organized dog events, prefer the clean, rounded effect of a powered nail sander. This operates in the same way as a household sanding tool and gives a smooth, snag-free finish to a dog's nails. It can prove more challenging to accustom a dog to the noise and feel of the sander, but it can be done if started early in his life.

Ask a professional groomer or veterinary assistant to demonstrate the proper way to clip your Staffy's nails. The more confident you are when handling your trimming tool, the easier the session will be.

Shampoo

Never use human shampoo—even baby shampoo—to bathe your Staffy. Even the mildest of them are too harsh for a dog's skin. They can strip the natural oils from the skin or cause an uncomfortable allergic reaction that warrants medical treatment. For the rare times when you need to bathe your Staffy, use a mild dog shampoo.

Dental Supplies

This is another situation in which the human versions of implements and products are unsuitable for dogs. Never use human toothpaste to brush a dog's teeth, for the same reason you shouldn't use it on a baby. Human toothpaste isn't meant to be swallowed, and neither babies nor dogs know how to spit it out. Special toothpaste formulated for dogs will not cause stomach upset or other illness if swallowed, and it tastes better. A dog isn't going to like wintergreen toothpaste as much as he will chicken or peanut butter flavor. Find a flavor he loves, and he will soon consider dental care to be a special treat!

The kind of toothbrush you use also contributes to the success of your canine dental care. Most dogs won't calmly sit with their mouths open while you brush their teeth, so you have to use a toothbrush with soft bristles and an easy-to-manipulate handle that allows you to quickly reach all tooth surfaces. A finger sheath is an alternative to a toothbrush that achieves the same cleaning effect. Made of pliable rubber or plastic, the sheath fits over your index finger. You put a dab of dog-flavored toothpaste on the textured surface and then rub your finger over the tooth surfaces. The nubbly texture removes plaque and food buildup.

BRUSHING

Thanks to his short, smooth fur, Staffy coat care is a breeze. For his regular brushings, a short, densely bristled brush with a comfortable handle is all you really need.

When brushing your Staffy, start at his head and work your way back toward the tail.

How to Brush Your Staffy

To brush your Staffy, start at his head and work your way back toward his tail. Brush hair in the same direction that it grows, being extra gentle on his sensitive underbelly and head. Use sufficient pressure to stimulate the skin but not so much pressure that you cause your dog any discomfort. If his skin twitches when you brush, you may be using too much pressure.

BATHING

Your Staffy will not require many baths during his lifetime. Exceptions occur when he gets into something nasty or is a working therapy dog who visits hospitals and nursing homes that frequently mandate baths prior to every visit. Regular brushing should be all he needs to stay shiny, healthy, and fresh. (Ahhh, that new dog smell…) Too much bathing can result in dry, itchy skin and a dull coat, just as when the wrong shampoo is used. If you feel strongly about bathing your Staffy on a regular basis, keep the frequency down to once a month, and be sure to use a mild shampoo formulated for dogs. Puppy shampoo is likely to be the mildest.

Where to Bathe Your Staffy

If the weather is sufficiently warm, you can bathe your Staffy outdoors. The advantage is obvious: You won't mess up your bathroom or laundry room. A plastic kiddy pool makes a great outdoor bathtub, especially when it's hard plastic versus the inflatable type. Nails or teeth can accidentally pierce the inflated plastic, turning your outdoor doggy spa into a flood zone. If you fill the pool from your garden hose, adjust the water temperature to a comfortable level by adding heated water, if necessary. Conversely, if the hose has been sitting outside in the hot sun, make sure that the water flowing from it isn't scalding. Have plenty of towels on hand to dry your Staffy as much as possible.

When an indoor bath is called for, choose a comfortably warm location that's free of drafts. The more comfortable and pleasant the environment, the more cooperation you can expect from your Staffy.

How to Bathe Your Staffy

Place a rubber mat on the floor of your tub or shower to give your Staffy surer footing and to prevent slips. Run the water until it's the right lukewarm temperature by testing on the inside of your arm to make sure that it's not too hot. It's too dangerous to let your Staffy jump into the tub, so carefully lift him in. Broad-chested breeds like the Staffy should be lifted with one arm around the front of the chest and the other arm around the back of the legs below the rump. Alternatively, you can support him with one arm underneath, just behind the front legs, and the other arm underneath, just in front of the rear legs, although one school of thought says this method of lifting puts too much stress on the internal organs. If you're unsure about how to safely pick up your Staffy, consult your vet. No matter how you pick up your Staffy, keep your grip secure but don't squeeze him too tightly.

Allow your Staffy a few minutes to get used to the feel of the water. If you have a handheld spray attachment, set the nozzle on a gentle spray and wet down his entire coat, shielding his eyes with your hand. If you don't have a sprayer, use a large plastic cup or bowl to pour bath water onto his body. Once his coat is wet, pour a quarter-sized dollop of dog shampoo into your palm and gently soap up the dog's body, avoiding his head. Work up a lather and gently massage it into his fur, remembering the underbelly and legs.

The head and face require careful attention. Even a little soap or water in the eyes or nose can turn bath time into an

Anal Sac Care

The anal sacs are two glands located on either side of a dog's anus that produce a smelly, brownish substance that facilitates elimination. Sometimes these sacs clog up, making your Staffy uncomfortable and at risk for infection. The classic symptom of anal sac impaction is when the dog scoots his bottom along the floor or ground, trying to ease the discomfort. He may also lick under his tail quite a bit. If the sacs are not emptied eventually, an abscess can form and possibly rupture through the skin. This condition is painful, messy, smelly, and warrants an immediate trip to the vet.

You can empty clogged anal sacs yourself if you have a strong stomach and someone to demonstrate the procedure, or the vet can do it. Your Staffy may never experience anal gland problems, but they are commonplace and easily treated.

Your Staffy only needs to be bathed once in a while or if he's rolled in something dirty.

unpleasant experience he won't forget by the next time he needs one. To clean his face, dampen a clean washcloth with warm water and carefully wipe around his eyes and nose. If soap does manage to find its way into his eyes, soothe the sting with a drop or two of mineral oil in the corner of each eye.

With the same washcloth, gently wipe his outer ears. Use a cotton ball dipped in mineral oil to gently clean inside the ear flap. Never stick a cotton swab or anything else down inside the ear—you could injure delicate tissues.

When it's time to rinse off, use the spray attachment or bowl to rinse away suds. Take care to remove all traces of soap. Shampoo residue will dull your dog's coat and may cause itching and flaking. Don't forget to rinse his underbelly and legs. This can be challenging without a spray nozzle, but it can be done. Gently splash cupfuls of fresh, warm water underneath, repeating as much as necessary to remove all the lather. If your Staffy will permit it, you can raise the front half of his body with your arm behind his front legs, exposing his underside. Be sure that his back feet are firmly planted on the tub mat, and keep a firm hold on him with your arm so that he doesn't feel unsteady or lose his balance. Then you can thoroughly rinse his belly and legs.

When the last bubbles have been rinsed clean and he's ready to exit the bath, brace yourself. The first thing he'll do when he's back on terra firma is to shake off all that excess moisture. You're probably already wet from assisting him in and out of the tub, so dress appropriately! Have a large towel ready to wrap him in, then briskly rub his body until barely damp. Lightly and carefully wipe his face to ensure that all soap and water are gone.

There you have it: Your spanking-clean Staffy is ready for his close-up. Remember to keep him away from any drafts or cold air until his coat is completely dry.

EAR CARE

To keep the inside of your Staffy's ears clean and comfortable, you'll want to perform a routine inspection, perhaps while you're brushing him. This enables you to spot any parasites, irritations, or discharge that could indicate a problem. Dogs who run through underbrush or in the woods should be checked for any burrs, cuts, or scratches around the ears.

How to Care for Your Staffy's Ears

Mineral oil is a great item to have on hand. In addition to easing the sting of irritated eyes, it works well as a gentle ear cleaner. Dip a cotton ball into a little of the oil and wipe away any surface dirt on the inside and outside of the ears. Try to reach into the nooks and crannies inside without poking way down inside the ear. If there's a deep-seated problem like ear wax, consult your vet. Without proper instruments and expertise, trying to clean deep inside the ear yourself is too risky to delicate tissues. It's best to let a veterinary professional handle it.

How do you know if there's a problem with your Staffy's ears? His behavior is a good communicator. If he repeatedly shakes his head, paws or scratches at an ear, or rubs his ears on the floor or carpet, something is causing him discomfort. Inspect the ears for redness, discharge, or unpleasant odor that could indicate inflammation or infection. A veterinarian will diagnose the problem and prescribe appropriate treatment, usually medicated ear drops to ease the itching and cure the infection. A liquid ear wash may also be prescribed to flush out bacteria and dirt and maintain a

Use a cotton ball dipped in a little mineral oil to wipe away any surface dirt on the inside and outside of the ears.

balanced pH level. Your vet can demonstrate exactly how to administer these treatments at home.

To use ear drops, gently hold the ear flap away from the head and drop the recommended dosage inside the ear. Replace the flap and gently rub the outside of the ear to work in the solution and minimize loss when he shakes his head. Dogs aren't always cooperative with this procedure, so it's helpful to have someone hold him still while you work on his ears.

EYE CARE

Although we may not think about a dog's eyes when it comes to routine health maintenance, they are an important part of your Staffy's ongoing care.

How to Care for Your Staffy's Eyes

The easiest step in caring for your Staffy's eyes is to check the home environment for any sharp or protruding objects at his eye level. Conduct a regular visual inspection of his eyes for any signs of irritation, infection, or injury.

Outdoor eye hazards come in the form of air pollution, thorny plants, and heavy underbrush. A Staffy owner should be aware that eye hazards can also come in the form of cruel humans who want to taunt the "pit bull" by throwing rocks or other objects at him over or through the fence. Vigilant supervision of your Staffy at all times is the best defense against injury.

Dogs can be afflicted by many of the same eye

Much "Adew" About Claws

Dewclaws are the vestigial nails by the fifth toe that sit on a dog's pasterns. They rarely make contact with the ground, so the nail isn't naturally kept short. Dewclaws have no real purpose, and most dog owners consider them a potential hazard because they can easily catch on tree roots, chain-link fences, or even indoor items like afghans or carpet and cause a very painful injury. Some countries, however, ban surgical dewclaw removal on the grounds that it's unnecessary mutilation, much like bans on ear cropping and tail docking.

Some dogs are born with dewclaws on only the front feet; some have them on all feet. If allowed to grow unchecked, the dewclaw can actually curl around the dog's leg and cut into his skin. Most breeders have the dewclaws removed when a puppy is two to five days old, while the dewclaws are so soft that they can be snipped off easily, without much discomfort. If the dewclaws remain intact after the puppy's first five days of life, it's best to wait until he's old enough to be safely anesthetized and have the dewclaws surgically removed. Removing the dewclaws of an adult dog means longer recovery time and an Elizabethan collar, a funnel-shaped plastic shield worn around the neck to prevent licking or chewing of the healing surgical site.

Unless you're a breeder, you probably won't need to worry about your Staffy's dewclaws, as they will have been removed long before he was old enough to go to a new home. If your rescued Staffy has intact dewclaws, remember to keep them trimmed short and eliminate as many potential "catching" places as possible from his home environment.

conditions as humans, including sties, allergies, infections, and cataracts. A healthy dog's eyes naturally secrete a clear mucus that is easily wiped away with a cotton ball or damp cloth. This mucus can discolor the area immediately underneath the eye, especially in light-colored dogs. Many dog-show participants use commercial wipes especially formulated to remove "tear stains." If the clear discharge turns bloody or yellow, consult a vet right away.

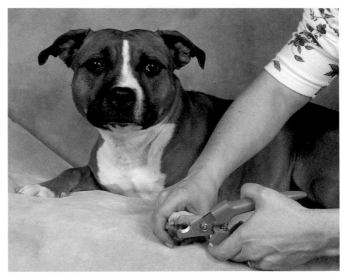

It's time to trim your dog's nails when you can hear them clicking on the floor when he walks.

Regular veterinary checkups are the best way to detect any serious eye problems like ingrown eye lashes or cherry eye, the prolapse of an eye gland. You want your Staffy's eyes to sparkle clear and bright for a lifetime.

NAIL TRIMMING

The long distances wild dogs covered during the day were enough to keep the nails worn down to a proper length. If your Staffy's nails aren't trimmed by nature, you need to make pedicures a regular part of his grooming regimen.

Why is it so important to keep toenails short? Nails allowed to grow too long will interfere with a dog's natural gait. He'll tend to put his weight on the back of his feet, which can cause an unappealing gait and splayed toes. Extremely long nails will eventually curl under the foot and puncture the toe pads. Long nails are also easily snagged on tree roots or other ground obstacles and can cause painful toe injuries.

How do you know when it's time to trim your Staffy's nails? If you can hear them clicking on the floor when he walks, it's time for a trim.

How to Trim Your Staffy's Nails

Before you begin trimming your Staffy puppy's nails, get him used to having his feet and toes handled. Play with them often, praising him when he doesn't pull away or resist. When you trim the first few nails and he behaves, reward with praise and a treat. He'll learn that if he endures you handling his toes, he'll receive good things.

The first thing to do before you start nail trimming is to locate the "quick," the blood vessel that runs through the center of each nail and grows relatively close to the nail end. The quick will bleed if accidentally cut, and this can be quite painful. Avoid cutting the quick at all costs. Your Staffy may forgive you once if you accidentally cut the quick, but do it again and he may head for the hills whenever he sees you open the supply drawer.

On white toenails, the red quick is easy to see and avoid. Still, you should err on the side of caution by cutting only the pointed tip of the nail. Allow for a margin of natural erosion during walking by staying well away from the quick. On black nails, the quick is difficult to see. You can identify it by shining a flashlight behind the nail when the paw is lifted. The quick will be shadowed darker than the rest of the backlit nail. Most people prefer to play it safe by cutting only a tiny bit of the nail or by using a file.

If you do cut the quick, your Staffy will let you know in no uncertain terms. Try to remain calm and stop the bleeding with a little styptic powder (available at drug stores) or cornstarch. In a pinch, you can also try pressing the bleeding nail into a soft bar of soap for a few seconds. Don't make a big deal out of it; this will only validate your Staffy's fears. Talk to him soothingly, and when he's calmed down, resume careful cutting with the next nail. The less of an issue you make it, the less of an issue it will be. End successful trimming sessions with lots of praise and a yummy treat.

DENTAL CARE

Dental hygiene is another of nature's tasks that we took over when we made dogs our companions. Canines in the wild consumed entire prey, including ligaments, bones, and cartilage, which naturally and effectively kept their teeth clean. Pet dogs who are fed commercial or home-cooked diets have tartar or plaque buildup on their teeth that must be removed by brushing. That's where we come in.

As with nail trimming, oral care is best begun early in puppyhood to acclimate the dog to the procedure. A strong adult Staffy who is determined that you are not sticking anything in his mouth besides food can engage you in a contest of wills. A puppy who learns to accept your fingers or a toothbrush in his mouth will grow into a cooperative adult.

How to Brush Your Staffy's Teeth

The first step in acquainting your Staffy with the tooth-brushing process is to get him comfortable with your fingers around and in his mouth. This won't be difficult because puppies will mouth just about anything within their reach. Approach him when he's calm, and stroke the outside of his cheeks with your fingers. This acts as a subliminal announcement that his mouth is about to be handled. Put a dab of dog toothpaste (not human toothpaste) on your finger and let him taste it. It's a very rare dog who doesn't enjoy the chicken or bacon flavors of most dog toothpastes.

At this point, you can move on to an actual toothbrush or finger sheath, which is a latex or plastic textured cover that fits over your finger and acts as the brushing instrument. Apply a small amount of toothpaste and start brushing only a few of the most accessible teeth at first. As his comfort level with the procedure increases, increase the number of teeth you brush until he allows you to do his whole mouth. Be sure to get the back molars where plaque tends to accumulate. Plan on about 30 seconds of brushing per side. When you're done, praise your Staffy to the skies so that he will look forward to the next dental cleaning.

Without regular brushing, plaque can accumulate on your dog's teeth and cause bad breath or worse. A full dental cleaning, where hardened plaque is scraped off teeth and from under the gum line, is performed by a vet while the dog is under general anesthesia to permit lengthy access to the dog's mouth. While the procedure itself isn't hazardous, general anesthesia carries inherent risks. Your dog should have an annual oral exam to determine if he needs a professional cleaning, but you can help keep serious problems from cropping up by faithfully seeing to your Staffy's oral health at home.

Chewing

Good canine oral care recognizes a dog's need to chew. Not just a phenomenon of teething puppies, chewing is an important component of a dog's physical and mental development. Chew toys are dragged around, scuffled over, and guarded with voiced warnings, all important life skills that puppies in the wild once needed to learn as pack positions evolved. If a young dog didn't learn how to defend his food against pilferage by littermates or more dominant pack members, he risked starvation. This instinct manifests today in dogs who let their "siblings" know in no uncertain terms that their food and chew toys are not for sharing.

Your Staffy should have an annual oral exam to determine if he needs a professional cleaning.

Chewing strengthens puppies' growing musculature and is also a way for them to explore the world and discern by taste and texture what is food and what isn't. Dogs can't always rely on their eyes to tell the difference between a garden snake and a garden hose.

When puppies start losing their baby teeth at around four months of age, the urge to chew intensifies, encouraging the adult teeth to come in and replace the baby teeth. Sometimes an adult tooth tries to break through before its puppy counterpart falls out. This is called a *retained deciduous tooth* and can cause infection if debris and hair become trapped between the baby tooth and emerging permanent tooth. This problem can be avoided with the help of appropriate chew toys, like Nylabones. As discussed in Chapter 3, the right chew toys are important to your Staffy's well-being and safety. Toys made of flimsy materials can be choked on or swallowed and can cause internal injury. The same is true for stuffed toys with button facial features or squeaky rubber toys. The buttons or beads of stuffed toys are easily ripped out and pose choking and intestinal hazards. The squeaker inside flimsy rubber or plastic toys is in danger of being removed and swallowed. Your best bet is to ask your vet what kinds of chew toys she recommends. Remember to monitor the condition of your Staffy's chew toys. If a toy or bone becomes splintered or develops rough edges from enthusiastic use, replace it.

The Senior Staffy's Mouth

By the time your Staffy reaches senior citizen status at around eight years or so, his teeth and gums may need special attention. If you notice the onset of bad breath and/or tartar buildup, it may be time for a professional cleaning at the vet's office, overall health permitting. (Because this procedure is performed while the dog is under general anesthesia, he must be in good general health to minimize the inherent, albeit unlikely, risk of death.) In addition to cleaning the teeth, the "dentist" will look for any chipped, cracked, or broken teeth and any signs of gum disease. Some older dogs develop hyperplasia, a condition in which fibrous extensions of gum tissue grow over the tooth and possibly interfere with the dog's bite. Even if the growth doesn't hinder the dog's bite, if allowed to proliferate, these tissue flaps can harbor bacteria and cause infection. Undetected and untreated, oral infection can become systemic, causing serious illness or even death. A full dental cleaning allows the vet to snip off these otherwise harmless gum tumors. Bleeding and pain are minimal, and your Staffy can resume eating the same day, consuming soft foods for a day or two.

Although some risk is involved with general anesthesia, the benefits of a

Fresh Breath

Once your Staffy outgrows the cute puppy-breath stage, you may need to sweeten his less-than-fresh mouth occasionally. First, let the vet determine that no underlying medical causes are present. If it's plain old halitosis, there are a few ways to solve the problem:

- commercial canine breath fresheners, usually chlorophyll drops or odor-neutralizing treats
- apple slices or fresh parsley sprigs, both of which have natural breath-freshening properties
- a full dental cleaning performed by the vet, followed by regular tooth brushing at home

The right chew toys are important to your Staffy's well-being and safety.

professional dental cleaning usually outweigh it. Routine oral health care at home and regular veterinary checkups will keep your Staffy smiling for years to come.

HOW TO FIND A PROFESSIONAL GROOMER

Extensive grooming is unnecessary because a Staffy's short, flat coat and sleek body stay beautiful with a minimum of care. Some dog owners, however, prefer to leave the occasional bath or toenail clipping to the experts.

Professional groomers work in veterinary clinics, pet supply stores, and even out of mobile units that come to your home to spruce up your dog. As with any professional who provides care or services to your Staffy, you want to find the very best. So how do you go about finding a good groomer?

First and foremost, you want a groomer who is sensitive to her canine clientele. Most groomers take up the profession because they enjoy being with dogs, but occasionally you'll see a groomer who is not happy in her work. Job dissatisfaction should not translate to rough handling of your dog. Even enthusiastic groomers can have a bad day, but they shouldn't vent their frustrations on the animals they groom.

Many franchised grooming facilities have large windows where customers can watch the groomers at work. Spend some time observing potential groomers of your Staffy. Do they treat their clients with compassion and respect, or do they handle the dogs in a way that makes you uncomfortable? If you notice a groomer mistreating or shouting at a dog, not only should you steer clear of her services, you should report your observations to the manager. In all likelihood, the store will rectify the issue rather than risk its professional reputation.

The logical place to start a search for any dog service is by referral. Ask fellow Staffy owners for a recommendation. Ask friends and neighbors with well-groomed dogs where they take their furry friends. You can also ask your vet to refer an outside groomer, although most veterinary practices provide basic grooming services like bathing and nail trimming, which is all the well-dressed Staffy needs. Owners of breeds like the Bichon Frise or Pomeranian need to find groomers experienced with the hair "style" their breeds dictate. Lucky Staffy owners have a simpler task: Find an experienced groomer who is compassionate with her clients and loves her job, and you're good to go.

If possible, check out the equipment your chosen grooming facility uses. If the staff will be bathing your Staffy, find out if the dryer has adjustable settings. Dryers hot enough to dry a Golden Retriever may be too hot for a Staffy. Ask what kind of shampoos and flea dips they use as well. You may want the latter product tested on a small area of your Staffy's skin to make sure that he doesn't have an allergic reaction.

A responsible Staffy owner is hands-on in every facet of her best friend's care. If you feel that a professional groomer can improve on your Staffy's perfection, you owe it to your dog to find the best.

While good grooming is important, it is not a remedy for ill health or poor physical fitness. If a Staffy is not well tended, no amount of brushing will disguise it. Grooming is part of the responsibility a dog owner undertakes. Fortunately for Staffy owners, regular grooming is easy and fast, leaving you lots of time to play ball with your handsome best friend.

TRAINING AND BEHAVIOR
of Your Staffordshire Bull Terrier

The Staffy's keen intelligence and desire to please make training a gratifying endeavor. Along with smarts and natural curiosity, the Staffy is a strong, sturdy dog who warrants training to show the world his many desirable qualities.

WHY TRAIN?

Responsible dog ownership means having control of your dog at all times. Although the adult "nanny dog" would never think of hurting a human child, a young and playful Staffy may not know his own strength. Proper training will enable you to curtail activities that may become too rough. Also, without mental stimulation, an intelligent dog like the Staffy can get into all sorts of mischief. Training is the perfect outlet for his quick mind and will give him the self-confidence every dog needs to thrive.

For the Staffy, proper training is especially important because of his unjustified notoriety as a member of the bully breed group that is so often deemed, albeit falsely, vicious. His manners must be impeccable lest he unjustly be accused of being "dangerous." As long as "pit bulls" continue to fall into the hands of people who foster aggression and fighting, who fail to properly socialize and train their dogs, and who indiscriminately breed their dogs, the Staffy and other bully breeds will continue to be slandered. Thorough training is the best defense against this libel.

Whether you plan to involve your Staffy in conformation, agility, or other activities or just want to cultivate a good family pet, the first order of business will be basic training. A well-mannered dog is fun to be around and lets you show off your impeccably mannered Staffy to people who may know nothing about the breed. He should learn that begging for food, exploring forbidden areas like the trash bin or Italian silk sofa, and jumping up on visitors are not acceptable. Teaching good manners is much easier than unlearning bad habits. In addition, basic training will establish your expectations for your dog and prepare him for any advanced training you may plan to pursue.

The good news is that Staffies are very trainable. The bond formed early between you and your Staffy will facilitate a relationship in which he understands what you expect of him and is happy to comply.

POSITIVE TRAINING

Positive training simply means rewarding a dog for doing something right and not rewarding him if he does something wrong. In no way is discipline to be interpreted as fear. In other words, you don't want to train your Staffy to obey you because he is afraid of the consequences if he doesn't. You want him to make the decision to obey you because he knows it will make you happy, and most likely, bring a reward in the form of a treat—thus reinforcing the desired action.

The idea of training by punishment for doing something wrong is nothing more than abuse. The dog will only learn to fear you, which can make his temperament unpredictable. He won't be able to discern what he is doing wrong from what he

Positive training rewards a dog for doing something right, often in the form of a treat.

should be doing right. Old-fashioned methods of "discipline," like rubbing a puppy's nose in a housetraining accident, don't teach him that eliminating in the house is bad. All he will know is that you are angry because he eliminated. Positive training is the only method of behavioral training you should practice.

HOW TO FIND A DOG TRAINER

The first step in obedience training is to find a reputable trainer to work with both you and your Staffy. Training is as much for the dog owner as it is for the dog because you'll be practicing at home what you learn during training sessions. Seek out a trainer who is compatible with your personality and philosophy.

Seek Referrals

Begin your search for a good dog trainer by seeking referrals. Your Staffy's breeder may also be a trainer or will certainly know of one she can recommend. You can also contact your local Staffordshire Bull Terrier club for a referral. If any of your friends or neighbors has a well-behaved dog, ask where she went for training. One thing you don't want to do is pick a name out of the phone book. Random selection is not a reliable way to choose a trainer for your Staffy. Proper training of an impressionable puppy is too important to leave to self-styled "experts."

Visit the Trainers

Once you have a few referrals, pay a visit to each one. Ask if you can observe a group training session—a reputable trainer will be happy to let you see for yourself what your Staffy could expect in her class. A good trainer uses a dog's very first teacher,

Group Classes or Private Lessons?

There are pros and cons to both group classes and individual obedience instruction. In a group setting, the dog must learn how to behave around distractions, namely the other dogs and people in the class. Because you want your Staffy to remain in your control at all times despite any distractions, this might be a good choice for you. Your dog may even find some future playmates among his classmates. The downside of group classes is that the distractions may prove too much for some dogs.

For dogs who have trouble staying focused, private classes may be in order. Sometimes a few one-on-one lessons are all a dog needs to join a group class later. Of course, individual lessons are also better for dogs with aggression or other behavioral issues. And sometimes private instruction is the only type of training busy dog owners can fit into their schedules.

A puppy or "kindergarten" class for Staffies between 10 and 16 weeks of age is part obedience training, part socialization. Here, owners also learn how to prevent problem behaviors and how to establish boundaries. All puppies stand to benefit greatly from kindergarten classes.

No matter which training environment you ultimately choose, be sure that there's a good fit among you, your Staffy, and the instructor. Observe different classes and different instructors, if possible. Make a mental note of your comfort level with each, and select the one you think is best for your purposes.

Find a dog trainer who is compatible with your personality and philosophy.

his mother, as a model. Your Staffy pup learned many things from his mother while he was still with her, and her teaching methods are good patterns for you to follow. She was fair, consistent, immediate, and appropriate in her discipline. Most importantly, she always acted out of love and concern for her pups. Even reprimands were meted out within a nurturing context.

Observe the demeanors of the "students." Are the dogs enjoying themselves? Does the trainer handle the dogs in a manner consistent with the way you want your Staffy treated? Are dogs and owners paying attention to the instructor? These are all important questions to ask yourself when seeking the right trainer for your precious Staffy. The right trainer will get the job done while making her students, canine and human, feel comfortable.

SOCIALIZATION

Socialization means acclimating your Staffy to the many people, animals, life situations, and environments that a dog will encounter in daily life. A puppy's socialization starts while he's still with his mother and breeder. Here is where he learns the basics of pack behavior and what his boundaries are. It's up to you, his new owner, to continue this all-important process.

How to Socialize Your Staffy

Take him with you everywhere possible: the park, on a walk downtown, to pet-friendly shops—any safe place you normally visit in everyday life. But remember that the world is a big and sometimes scary place to a little pup. While he should learn as much as possible about the world he inhabits, keep in mind that loud noises, bright flashing lights, and large vehicles can frighten him. Forego taking him to the Independence Day fireworks or the stock car races. Such environments can be scary to even well-socialized adult dogs.

Proper socialization also means introducing your Staffy to all kinds of people in all kinds of situations, as well as to other animals. Allow him to interact with people of different races, genders, and ages. This won't be hard, as everyone you meet will want to stop and admire your adorable Staffy pup. Encourage interaction with people in wheelchairs, on crutches, and using walkers. Introduce him to other pets while under your careful supervision. The socialization he receives up to three months of age will largely determine his impressions of the world around him. A puppy who isn't socialized can grow into a fearful or aggressive dog. Presenting a friendly, affectionate, well-mannered Staffy to the community will go a long way toward dispelling the misconceptions about bully breeds. Besides, it will give you an excuse to show off your newest family member and give him the loving attention every dog craves.

CRATE TRAINING

The dog crate is not a jail cell; it's a safe, cozy place your Staffy can call his own, where he can eat, sleep, relax, and travel in security. Unfortunately, some people harbor the notion that crating is cruel and unnatural to social animals like dogs. People who believe that dogs should have freedom at all times are not taking into consideration the denning instinct. Dogs instinctively want to be in protected, sheltered nooks. This is

Socializing your Staffy puppy includes safely introducing him to other dogs.

why we see dogs curling up for a nap at the base of a stairway or underneath a table. The crate is a place of refuge that protects the dog from environmental dangers. An unsupervised puppy who is allowed to roam the house at will is at serious risk. Toxic houseplants, chemicals, electric cords, and even furniture and steps all pose safety hazards to a curious little puppy who will chew on anything. Crate training isn't cruel; it's responsible dog ownership.

The Benefits of Crate Training

When a puppy is about five weeks old, he'll start wandering away from his mom and littermates to eliminate. He is acting on an instinct not to soil his living area. Combined with a properly used crate, this instinct will actually facilitate housetraining.

Crate Caveat

Never use the crate as a form of punishment. You want your Staffy to enjoy being in his crate, safe and sound.

By taking advantage of his instinct to keep his living area clean, you can readily teach your Staffy pup where you want him to relieve himself. Most puppies, though, go to their new homes around ten weeks of age, long before they have full bowel and bladder control. He won't be able to go for more than an hour or so without a potty break. So even when crate training is accomplished and your puppy understands that he shouldn't soil his crate, you must be sure not to leave him in it too long. A puppy who is crated immediately after elimination and not given any more food or water should be able to go for, at most, two hours without soiling. Adults vary in how long an individual dog can "hold it," but in general, an adult dog should be taken out of his crate for a potty break after four or five hours, except at bedtime.

There will be times when you are unable to closely watch your puppy, even while you're at home together. This is another time when the crate proves very useful. It will keep him safe from mischief and danger and prevent him from soiling all over the house. If he balks at being in the crate and away from you, try putting the crate in a location where he can see you move about. Sometimes your reassuring presence is all he wants.

Location, Location, Location

Placement of your Staffy's crate can mean the difference between a decent night's sleep and long hours of vocal unhappiness. Try putting the crate in your bedroom, near your bed. Knowing you are close by will comfort the puppy and reduce crying. If he whimpers or scratches at the crate door during the night, most likely he needs to relieve himself. By taking him outside right away, you reinforce the housetraining message and bring closer that night of undisturbed sleep. When he eliminates outside where you want him to, praise him. Return him immediately to his crate, saying "Bed" or "Crate."

Puppies nap often throughout the day. When you see your Staffy getting ready for a snooze, put him inside the crate and shut the door. He'll get the idea that the crate is the place for sleep, and a cozy place at that!

The crate is a dog's special refuge, a safe place he can call his own. He should be able to retreat there to get away from the hustle and bustle of family life whenever he wants to. Children should never follow a puppy or dog to his crate and try to play with him or pull him out. Nor should a child try to fit herself into the dog's crate. It's not a playhouse and not a toy. The crate is your Staffy's private suite and should always remain so.

Size Does Matter

Although your Staffy pup will eventually grow into an adult dog who needs an adult-sized crate, it's not a good idea to start off with a crate that large. A crate that is too big will make it easy for the puppy to soil at one end without compromising his bedding at the other. This can hamper your housetraining efforts. It's better to start with a smaller crate and upsize it as he grows. A good rule of thumb for determining proper crate size is that it should be large enough for the dog to stand up and turn around in comfortably. If you

The crate is a safe, cozy den that your Staffy can call his own.

Training will help your dog become a well-behaved member of the family.

really don't want to invest in different-size crates while your Staffy's growing, you can partition off a large crate, giving the puppy only half as his entire living space. This will deter him from soiling his bed. Relocate the partition to afford him more room as he grows.

How to Crate Train Your Staffy

It may take a puppy a little while to understand that the crate is his own safe haven, so it's a good idea to introduce him to it before you actually need to confine him in it. Make the crate comfortable by lining the bottom with thick layers of newspaper. This will do double duty as a cushiony surface on which to relax and an absorbent pad for any accidents that take place in the crate. Once the crate is comfortably appointed with the newspapers and a toy or two, prop open the crate door and toss a treat inside while you say "Crate" or "Bed." Let him wander inside on his own, sniff around, take the treat, and exit at will. If he doesn't go inside right away, don't push him. Give him time to decide when he wants to enter the crate and accept the treat. This will show him that the crate is a nice place, not a prison. Repeat this scenario several times daily until he enters the crate without hesitation.

Once he's used to the crate itself and comfortable being in it, serve his next meal inside, leaving the door open while he eats. Again, don't force him inside or make a big deal over it. Let him wander in when he's ready to eat. When he seems accustomed to eating his meals there, the next step is to close the crate door while he eats. Stay close by, and let him out as soon as he's finished so he can take an outdoor potty break. Before long, he'll realize that the crate isn't a place of punishment or deprivation but a cozy den where good things can be had.

Bedtime is a little more difficult. Your Staffy pup will no doubt cry the first night or two that he spends away from his mother, littermates, and the only home he's ever known. This is normal, but it's hard for the new owner who must listen to a puppy's pitiful cries during the night! Other than taking him outside to eliminate once or twice during the night, resist the temptation to take him out and comfort him when he cries. If you give in, he will learn that crying yields the desired results. Instead, say "Quiet!" in a firm voice if he starts crying as soon as he is put to bed. Or simply leave the room and close the door. Difficult as it is, you must convey to the puppy that he is taken out of his crate only when he's quiet and you're ready.

HOUSETRAINING

Easily the number-one goal of new puppy owners, housetraining is one of the most readily accomplished training tasks. It's waiting for the puppy's immature organs to catch up that can be frustrating!

You can start teaching your Staffy pup where it's appropriate for him to relieve himself as soon as you bring him home with you. But be patient; some puppies mature later than others and require more time to learn. Be consistent, and your smart Staffy should pick up on it in no time.

How to Housetrain

Housetraining your new Staffy can begin as soon as you bring him home. When you pick him up at the breeder's, scoop up some dirt or shavings soaked with his littermates' urine and put it in a sealable plastic bag. Once home, scatter it around the outdoor spot you've picked as a designated elimination area. The scent of his littermates' urine will identify the site to your puppy as the appropriate place to relieve himself. If you don't have access to scented shavings or dirt, the puppy's first elimination in his newly designated potty area will serve to mark the spot.

Paper Training

Some dog owners prefer to begin the housetraining process with paper training, which is teaching the puppy to relieve himself on spread newspapers in a designated indoor area. This makes sense for apartment dwellers who can't always dash outside with a puppy before an accident happens. If possible, however, it's better to skip paper training and go directly to fostering outdoor bathroom habits. Your Staffy may become confused if you teach him to go on paper and then switch to a different environment.

As soon as you arrive home with your Staffy, go immediately to the outdoor potty place. Put him down where you've spread the urine scent, if possible, and wait until he urinates and/or defecates. This may take some time, so be patient. Lavish praise on him when he goes. Make him believe he's performed the greatest feat ever.

As your Staffy settles into your life together at home, watch for tell-tale signals that he needs to eliminate. If he walks around in circles, sniffing the floor, he's searching for that familiar scent to tell him he's in the right place to go. Take him directly outside and praise him when he relieves himself. Always take him outside directly after eating, drinking, or sleeping, and heap praises on him when he goes in the right place.

Accidents Happen

It's a fact of life, so don't be surprised when your new puppy makes mistakes in the house. Don't punish him for it. He will think you're angry because he eliminated, not because he eliminated in the wrong place. The only thing he'll come away with is a distrust of you, which is not the message you want to convey.

Positive training is the only way to teach your pup the difference between indoor accidents and outdoor elimination. If you catch your Staffy in the act of soiling inside the house or crate, say "No" in a firm voice and take him outside immediately to finish the job. This may take a few minutes, as the interruption is distracting. When he finally goes, praise lavishly to show your approval of this bathroom spot.

If you discover the accident after the fact (usually by stepping in it), it's too late for damage control. If you chastise him now for something he did earlier, he won't make the connection and won't understand why you're upset with him. Chalk it up to experience, and clean up the mess right away with a product made to neutralize the smells in urine and feces. Ordinary cleaning products may kill germs and prevent or remove stains, but they do nothing to eliminate the identifying scent. If the stain penetrated the carpet and soaked the padding underneath, the odor will still mark the spot, even though the stain is removed. If your home is carpeted, and you aren't sure where

Take your puppy outside to eliminate at regular, frequent intervals.

accidents have happened, you may want to invest in a handheld black light. Available in pet supply stores, a black light used in a completely darkened room will show up even old urine stains, revealing exactly where the accidents occurred so that you can neutralize the odor.

Above all, remember that puppy accidents in the house are really your fault, not his. It means that, at some point, your supervision lapsed. Clean up the accident and carry on. It may take your Staffy several months before he is physically able to "hold it" for more than an hour or two, but he'll understand fairly quickly that you want him to go only in certain places. Be patient and consistent, and before long you'll have a successfully housetrained Staffy.

BASIC TRAINING TOOLS

Every successful endeavor needs the proper tools, and training your Staffy is no exception. In researching dog training and the required implements, you are likely to find many different opinions on which tools are necessary, especially if the opinions are marketing a specific product. The truth is that you won't need elaborate and expensive training paraphernalia, much of which is designed for restraint and punishment, not positive reinforcement. The hands-on tools you'll need for productive training can be found in any store, with the widest varieties found in pet supply stores. We already possess the most important tools: love, gentleness, patience, and a positive attitude. Add a healthy, happy Staffy to the mix, and training will be a fun, gratifying experience.

Collar

Any kind of collar will feel strange to a puppy until he gets used to it. He will paw and scratch at it and try to wiggle his head out of it, but eventually he will adjust.

For everyday use, an adjustable buckle collar is best. It should fit comfortably around your Staffy's neck, not so loose that he can slip his head out of it but not so tight that his throat is constricted. Flat nylon buckle collars come in a rainbow of colors and styles, allowing you to decide what your well-dressed Staffy will be wearing this season.

For conformation training and showing, the most popular collar choices seem to be the thin nylon show collar and the fine chain collar. These should be used only for training sessions. Not only does that signal to the dog that it's time for "school," but the chain type of collar is too risky for everyday use. It can easily catch on all kinds of objects and cause injury or even strangle the dog. Prong and pinch collars are not recommended, and in some areas, not allowed.

Leash/Lead

A nylon, leather, or cotton-webbing training leash (also called a lead) about 6 feet (2 m) long is a popular choice for training sessions with your Staffy. Some leashes are made entirely of chain links, but many dog handlers find them uncomfortable to work with. They tend to be heavy and catch on too many things to be practical. Retractable leashes, in which a winding mechanism automatically lengthens and retracts the thin leash according to the dog's pace, are popular for nontraining walks but not the best choice for the powerful adult Staffy. If he decides to take off after something he sees, his momentum can snap the line right out of the plastic housing.

If you find a leash cumbersome, or if it's too

Your puppy needs a leash about 6 feet (2 m) long for training.

flimsy to hold up against the dog, it won't do you much good. Remember that a Staffy who is habitually off-leash outdoors before you've cemented your position of control may not obey you. If he sees or smells something too enticing to resist, all training progress will disappear. If you want to give your young Staffy some freedom in a safe, enclosed area but

Bite-sized treats work best when training.

don't trust him to obey, let him explore with the leash attached to his collar but hanging free of your hand. Remain close by so that you can pick it up and regain control if you need to.

The purpose of a leash is to keep the dog in your control at all times. No matter which leash you use for which purpose, it's important that you and your dog both feel comfortable using it.

Treats

The expression "will work for food" is never more applicable than in dog training. Trainers always have on hand a stash of wholesome, easy-to-store and -swallow treats. Even well-trained veteran show dogs respond to the motivation of treats in the show ring. Bits of hotdog, cheese, or cooked chicken all make excellent training rewards. Dry biscuits don't make the best training treats because they take too much time to eat. By the time your Staffy has finished chewing a hard biscuit, he will have forgotten why he received it to begin with.

Treats can also be used to mark a behavior. The dog will soon learn to associate the behavior with reward, and he'll repeat that behavior to see if a yummy tidbit is in his future.

Treat Randomly

Believe it or not, treats in training have a downside. If you consistently reward good performance with treats, your Staffy may decide that he won't perform without them. You can prevent this problem by having him perform a couple of commands *before* rewarding him with a treat. Slowly increase the number of nontreat-rewarded commands, then vary their order: two *sits* for a chunk of cheese one day, a *sit-stay* and a *down* for a bite of hotdog the next. Once your Staffy realizes that no established pattern exists for treat rewards, he will probably do your bidding the first time in the hope that it may result in one. Ultimately, you want him to do your bidding primarily because he wants to please you.

The Treat Myth

An old school of thought says that treat rewards will encourage a dog to beg at the table. In truth, the only way to encourage begging at the table is to give food from the table. Treats should be passed out well away from the family's dinner table. Your smart Staffy will know that praise and tasty treats are associated with good behaviors that make his owner happy.

LEASH TRAINING

Although it may not seem obvious, leash training is one of the first things you and your new Staffy should learn. (Leash training can be accomplished simultaneously with basic obedience training or can be a prelude to it.) As a young pup, he won't wander far from you, nor

Children and Puppies

Children under the age of six typically don't understand the implications of certain behaviors toward animals. A toddler who wants to give a puppy a loving pat on the head may actually smack the unsuspecting pup too hard. Or a child may push away a puppy who is play-biting or nipping her, which the pup may interpret as a game and come back for more. Also, a child should never try to pull a puppy out of his crate or attempt to fit herself inside the crate. The pup will never develop the sense of security in his crate that is necessary for successful crate training.

It's crucial that adults closely supervise all interactions between kids and dogs. Only when they learn respect and love for each other can harmony reign.

would you allow him to. But he'll become more adventurous as he matures, and you'll need to protect him from cars, other dogs, and the myriad dangers of the big bad world. And because an adult Staffy is a strong, muscular dog, he could easily pull you along on a walk if he isn't trained to match his pace to yours. Also, leash training is a must if you plan to show your Staffy in conformation or participate in any other organized dog activities.

A puppy is old enough to start leash training by seven weeks of age, when he has developed enough stamina for short walks. His attention span will also have increased by then to the point where he will benefit from some mental stimulation.

How to Leash Train

To teach a puppy how to walk nicely on a leash, you must first teach him to follow you off leash. Put on his training collar, attach the lead, and begin walking in a calm area like your backyard, allowing him to explore at will. While he's happily investigating the area, show him a treat and call him to come to you. Most puppies gladly come running when they are called. Praise him when he does, and give him the treat. Encourage him to follow as you walk for a few minutes, then allow him to explore some more on his own.

To teach a puppy to walk nicely on leash, first teach him to follow you off leash.

Your goal is to familiarize him with walking at your side off leash, so the transition to walking on leash with you will be natural.

Once he's gotten the hang of walking with you off lead, it's time to try it on lead. Do this in the same area so that the puppy will smell familiar scents and stay focused. A new area with unfamiliar smells just begging to be explored is too distracting. Attach the leash to the collar and begin walking. Call the puppy to you, showing him the treat, and he should follow as he did off leash. An alternate method is to attach the lead to the puppy's collar, then back away from him with a treat in your hand. Stoop down and offer the treat as you call him to come. This sends two important messages: He should come to you when called, and following you will reap rewards. As always, praise generously when he performs well.

(To teach your dog to heel, or walk by your side, see section "Heel.")

BASIC OBEDIENCE

Because you've made a conscious decision to add a Staffy to the family, it's understood that you've read up on the breed and talked to professionals about its specific needs. Even a naturally affectionate breed like the Staffy must learn the boundaries of obedience, especially in light of the many misconceptions about

the breed's temperament. Basic obedience training should begin within the first few weeks of his arrival at his new home, so preparation is a must.

First, understand what to expect from your Staffy during training. Puppies have very short attention spans, so keep initial training sessions down to ten minutes. Conduct several identical sessions throughout the day so that he gets the benefit of repetition without much distraction.

It bears repeating that positive reinforcement for a desired behavior, rather than chastisement for mistakes, is the key to successful training. Punishment is not only confusing and ineffective, it's unfair. The dog hasn't yet learned what is right before he is punished for doing something wrong.

Before you begin training your Staffy, consider your goals for him. Do you want a calm, polite family pet? Do you anticipate working as a therapy dog? Do visions of a career in organized sports dance in your head? The type of training can vary as much as the desired activity, but the basic obedience lessons you teach first are at the heart of it all.

Sit

The simple *sit* is invariably the first command a dog learns. It's a good place to start because a puppy already knows how to do it. The trick is to get him to do it when you want him to do it. When he learns how to sit still, he learns that consequences to his actions occur if he doesn't control himself. You can then use his mastery of the *sit* to your advantage for other lessons. No matter how long it takes him to learn other commands, if you end each training session with a nicely executed *sit*, followed by a treat, you'll keep up his confidence and make obedience training a happy experience.

How to Teach Sit

In preparation for a training session, put on your Staffy's training collar and leash. Hold the leash in your left hand and a food treat in your right. Hold your hand with the treat by his nose, and allow him to lick it but not take it. At this point, you're just introducing him to the incentive. Say "Sit" and slowly raise your food hand from in front of his nose upward to over his head. He will automatically assume a *sit* position as his eyes and head rise to follow the treat's path. Give the verbal command at precisely the same moment that his head goes up and his rear goes down. Give him the treat, and lavish praise on him.

The sit *command is often the first command a dog learns and is a good building block for other skills.*

Remember, Staffies love nothing better than making their humans happy, so he will quickly learn this command. Once he does, wean him away from food treats the majority of the time when he sits on command, but keep up the hearty praise. There will come a time in his life when you do not have treats on hand but need your dog to obey.

Stay

Arguably the most important basic command, you want the *stay* order obeyed with all the gusto a Staffy can muster. Don't skimp on mastering this command; the *stay* could one day prevent him from engaging in a serious altercation or getting into the path of an oncoming vehicle. The challenge is teaching it to a puppy who wants to be by your side every minute. During leash training, you've taught him to follow you; how do you now tell him to be at some distance from you and stay there?

How to Teach Stay

What Is Compulsive Training?

Compulsive training is a correction-based method that forces a dog to obey. It is usually used with military and law enforcement dogs. Most pet owners deem the method "unnecessary roughness" and turn to other training methods. The goal of obedience training is for the dog to make a conscious decision to obey you, not because he fears the consequences if he doesn't.

Begin with the puppy in a *sit*, next to your left leg. Keep his head slightly raised with gentle pressure on the leash, which you hold in your left hand. Have a treat in your right hand, holding it in the fold between your thumb and forefinger, and place that hand at your Staffy's nose. Tell him "Stay," making a *stop* gesture with the four fingers of your open right palm in front of his face. Step forward with your right foot and stand directly in front of the dog, releasing pressure on the leash. Let him lick the treat in your right hand so that he stays focused on the reward, and keep his head facing upward to maintain the *sit* position. Count to five, then turn back around to stand next to him again, with the dog on your left. As soon as you are back in your original position, give him the treat and lots of praise. He stayed, even if it was just for five seconds.

If your Staffy steps out of his *sit* position when you move away, stop him and start the lesson over by putting him back in a sit. He may not get this one right away since it combines the use of verbal and hand signals, but try not to get frustrated. Keep the practice sessions short, and always end with a *sit*, praise, and a treat reward.

As your Staffy becomes adept at the *stay* command, gradually increase the time you ask him to hold the position. Keep in mind, though, that if he is not holding the *stay* and moving too much, you may be asking him to hold it for longer than he is ready. Go back to the beginning and reteach the basic *stay*.

Heel

Heeling occurs when a dog walks beside his human on a

leash without pulling. Because of the Staffy's natural strength, the *heel* is an important command to learn. You want to walk your dog, not have him walk you. It may take some time for him to fully understand that the human doesn't proceed unless the dog is calmly heeling.

Training to heel actually begins when the young puppy learns to follow his human while walking off leash. When he's ready to move on to on-leash walking, you're ready to begin teaching the *heel*.

How to Teach Heel

Put your Staffy in the *sit* position, next to your left foot. With the leash in your left hand, step off with your left foot. As you make the first step, say "Heel." If he doesn't step forward as you do, encourage him to move by slapping the coils of extra leash against your leg as you keep walking. Walk together about three steps; stop and tell him "Sit." Praise him verbally, holding your position as he holds his. After a moment, say "Heel" again and take three more steps. Stop again and have him sit.

As long as he stays by your left leg while walking, praise him. If he stops or veers away, stop walking and start the lesson over. Your immediate goal is to have him walk nicely beside you for three steps, without pulling on the leash. When he has mastered heeling for three steps, advance to five. Keep increasing the number of steps you take, with him heeling, until he understands that leash walking means heeling.

Sometimes a particularly stubborn dog will continue pulling on his leash. If

Heeling occurs when a dog walks beside his human on a leash without pulling.

When teaching the down command, say "Down" and slowly lower a treat to his front feet to lure him into position.

your Staffy is one of them, stand still and don't move until he stops pulling and resumes the proper heeling position. Eventually, he'll get the message. If he doesn't, put off the lesson for another time. End the session with a *sit* so that the last thing he does is obey your command, thus ending on a positive note.

Down

This command requires a puppy to lie down on his belly and stay there. Initially, he may feel vulnerable in this position, so you must take care to use the proper method of teaching the *down*.

How to Teach Down *From a* Sit

With training collar and lead attached, put your Staffy in the *sit* position. Hold the leash in your left hand and a treat in your right. Rest one hand lightly on top of his shoulders. Do not push down on his back; just let your hand rest there to guide him close to your side when he lies down. Move your right hand in front of his nose and say "Down" very quietly, slowly lowering the treat to his front feet. When your hand reaches the floor, keep it moving forward along the floor in front of the dog. He will try to follow the food hand by lowering himself to the floor. Talk softly to him all the while; your reassuring voice will lower any anxiety.

When your dog's elbows reach the floor, give him the treat and soft praise. Try to keep him in the *down* position for a few seconds. Everything should be done in a soothing, easy way to reassure him. If you pull the treat away too far and too fast, he'll stand up instead of lying down. If you push your hand down on his body and speak sternly, he'll feel threatened and unwilling to obey. Be patient until he does what you want. When he's comfortable with the command, take the treat out of the scenario but continue using your right hand for a signal. Eventually, he will know that the downward hand movement, coupled with the verbal command, means "hit the deck."

How to Teach Down From a Stand

Teaching your Staffy to obey the *down* command from a standing position is not much different from the *sit* position. Say "Down" and lower the hand with the treat to the floor. He will lower his forelegs into a play bow, and then you can slowly move the treat on the floor toward you, away from his legs. The complete motion your treat hand makes is like tracing a capital letter "L." As soon as the rear end is down, give the treat and lots of praise.

Later on, you can practice the *down-stay*, in which he remains in the *down* position until released by a verbal command from you, usually something like "Okay" or "Release."

Come

Surprisingly, the *come* command is more involved than you'd think. It doesn't take much for your Staffy pup to come to you when called, but as adolescence approaches, distractions in the form of tantalizing odors in the grass will override his eagerness to come to you when called. *Come* is easily taught but can just as easily be untaught if misapplied.

How to Teach Come

There are two simple ways to teach your

Let Me Hear Your Body Talk...

A dog's body language can tell you a lot once you know what to look for.

Body Language	What It Means
Dog looks at you sideways with a lowered head.	"I'm unsure of your next move and I'm worried."
Dog stares at you with an upright head, standing on tiptoes.	"I'm equal to the challenge and ready to pounce."
Front half of dog's body is lowered in a bow.	"Let's play!"
Dog's entire body is crouched, with tail hanging down and ears folded back.	"I submit to you."
Dog's lips are curled back, fangs visible.	"Be warned!"
Fur down the center of dog's back stands on end.	"I'm afraid but ready to defend myself if necessary."

puppy to come. One way is to have the pup on a long lead while you stand at the far end of it. Gradually gather the leash in your hands to bring him toward you while calling "Come!" He'll no doubt trot happily toward you, so start praising him as soon as he starts to move. Even if he gets distracted before he reaches you and veers off toward something else, praise the steps he did take when you gave the *come* command. Most of the time, he will successfully reach you, and literally every step in the right direction is deserving of praise. Always reinforce positive actions, however brief.

Another, more realistic method of teaching the *come* is to kneel down, hold your arms wide open, and enthusiastically call "Come!" Praise your Staffy to the skies when he comes running to you. You won't need to use a treat to lure him, but you can use one to teach him that *come* doesn't mean "Come knock me over." When the rapidly approaching Staffy is about three lengths away from mowing you down, give the *sit* command with a treat in the outstretched hand. When he stops to investigate the treat, move your food hand upward over his muzzle to put him in a *sit*. If he jumps up for the treat, you're holding your hand too high. Put him back in a *sit* before repeating the *come* exercise.

There are a few important points to remember about this command:

- Never call your Staffy to come to you and then punish him. Association of the *come* command with anything negative unravels all training progress in an instant.
- Don't overwork the command by calling him to you too often.
- Spring an unexpected "Come!" on your Staffy when he is distracted by another activity, like playing. Your goal for him is to learn to heed your call no matter what else he may be doing.
- Always reward him for coming to you, whether it's in the form of a treat or very enthusiastic praise and attention.

PROBLEM BEHAVIORS

The very intelligence and tenacity that make the Staffy such a wonderful breed are the same qualities that can be troublesome if you aren't prepared to deal with them. We should remember, though, that many of what we consider problem behaviors come naturally to dogs, such as barking, digging, chewing, jumping on people, and yes, drinking out of the toilet. (Let's face it: It does look like a huge water bowl.) The good news is that once problem behaviors are identified, they can usually be controlled.

Problem behaviors are the number-one cause of pet abandonment, but training and patience can help prevent and control many of these behaviors. You owe it to your Staffy to try to understand the underlying causes of behaviors that we might find distasteful but come naturally to dogs. We shouldn't expect dogs to stop being dogs just because they live with humans. In fact, if humans acted a little more like dogs, the world would be a more joyful place!

Aggression

While Staffies are not aggressive to humans, they have a certain genetic tendency toward dog aggression. Young adult Staffies may develop the urge to match their strength against other dogs. The best way to circumvent this instinct is through early and ongoing socialization. The well-socialized Staffy learns early in life that other dogs are not necessarily threatening. Training him to ignore other dogs can be taken to a level where the Staffy will ignore even a dog who challenges him.

Aggression is not merely a dose of bad manners. It's a potentially dangerous situation for a powerful, independent

Once problem behaviors are identified, they can usually be controlled.

breed like the Staffy. With the reputation for viciousness that the bully breeds already endure, the last thing you want is an unpredictable Staffy who makes people—even his own family—afraid of him.

Solution

First and foremost, realize that you will need professional help with an aggression problem. Even the most self-confident Staffy owner shouldn't attempt to solve this issue alone. Seek the help of a vet and/or a dog behaviorist, both of whom can help you identify the cause of the problem. As a team, hopefully you can work out a program together to recondition an aggressive Staffy.

If your Staffy thinks he is in charge of the pack (your family and pets), his body language will tell the tale. A dog ready to challenge another dog will make and maintain direct eye contact and make himself appear as large as possible by holding his tail high, his chest out, and his ears erect. He may also assume a "stalking" posture, with head down and body somewhat close to the ground.

Aggression may also stem from fear. The "fight or flight" instinct kicks in, and the dog faces down whatever or whoever is scaring him. The fear may be rooted in inadequate socialization during puppyhood or a traumatic experience. If you can isolate the cause of a dog's fear, you can recondition his response to it.

Don't allow anyone to approach your Staffy without first asking your permission. This gives you the chance to put him in a *sit* and prepare to receive the attention. He's less likely to be frightened of something that doesn't come as a surprise. Praise him when he behaves well. If he hints at any aggressive behavior, correct him verbally and immediately remove him from the situation.

Fear-oriented aggression can also affect an injured dog in pain. This is why many canine first-aid books advise muzzling an injured dog before attempting to transport him. If your Staffy is hurting, you'll most likely know about it, but sometimes painful injuries are invisible. Only a thorough veterinary examination can rule out any physical reasons behind uncharacteristic aggression.

Barking

Barking is the only means dogs have of talking. We don't always know what they're trying to say, which can be frustrating. We may not know if they're scared, happy, or angry. Eventually, you will become familiar with your Staffy's unique vocalizations in different situations, but what do you do if his barking becomes excessive?

Solution

You should never punish your dog for barking. There are situations when you would *want* him to bark, such as if there were an intruder or a fire. Unfortunately, a dog can't discern for himself when it's appropriate to bark and when it isn't. Only if the barking is habitual, excessive, and unexplainable should you take steps to correct it.

Staffies are not known to be problem barkers, but any dog left alone for long periods may discover that barking brings attention, even if it's a neighbor yelling for him to cease and desist. You can encourage your Staffy to be quiet when he's at home with you. If he begins barking for no apparent reason, tell him "Quiet!" and reward him when he stops. Once he appears to respond well to the command, take the training a step further. Go for a walk around the block by yourself, listening for any barking as you depart and return. Make exits and entrances uneventful to deter barking out of excitement. If your Staffy

Dogs left alone for long periods may discover that barking brings attention.

If your Staffy is chewing on inappropriate objects, distract him with a chew toy.

does bark, tell him "Quiet!" and repeat the exercise until he virtually ignores your comings and goings. The final step is to ask a neighbor to come out and talk to you in the street. If your Staffy barks because he's missing the party, correct him by saying "Quiet!" Repeat these exercises as often as necessary until he learns that you don't want him to bark indiscriminately.

Chewing

Destructive chewing is usually a problem behavior of puppies who can and will chew anything. Teething lasts until approximately six months of age, and the chewing urge intensifies during this period. The danger is not only limited to toxicity or digestive tract injury, but the puppy who chews on a live electric cord risks death. The plastic coating on the wires is a tempting chewy delight, so removing them from the puppy's environment is imperative. Hide electric cords under carpeting, or affix them to the baseboards with a staple gun. Don't forget to provide plenty of safe chew toys so that he won't be tempted by household items.

An adult dog who exhibits destructive chewing behavior may suffer from separation anxiety. Such dogs are known to gnaw on door jambs and furniture. Or, he could be chewing out of boredom. Solving the problem means identifying the cause and working to correct it.

Solution

Puppies not only like to chew; they need to chew. Providing plenty of safe, size-appropriate chew toys is the best way to redirect a puppy's chewing behavior. Many chew toys have varied flavors to tempt the palate and textured surfaces to help clean teeth and gums. Just make sure that you select ones that won't splinter, break, or tear. During teething, freeze a wet washcloth and allow your Staffy pup to gnaw on it. The cold will soothe sore gums.

Bored dogs may be placated with chew toys that offer some mental stimulation, such as a hard ball that dispenses treats through openings when the ball is in motion. Or, spread a little peanut butter inside a hollow chew bone. The task of getting at all the filling can occupy your dog for a long while.

To ensure that your Staffy steers clear of chewing on certain objects, apply a little bitter apple spray to furniture legs or anything else you don't want chewed. It's a safe but unpleasant-tasting liquid available at any pet supply store.

Safety is the primary concern with chewers, especially those who chew out of separation anxiety. Consult your vet about options for dealing with this issue, but meanwhile, protect your Staffy from chewing something potentially dangerous by crating him while you're out. If he's properly crate trained, this shouldn't be a problem. If he's still in the process of crate training and hasn't yet learned to like a room of his own, grit your teeth and crate him anyway. His safety must take precedence over his temporary unhappiness during your brief absence.

Coprophagia

Coprophagia, or the eating of feces, is one of the dog's more disgusting behaviors. Like it or not, though, it is a behavior perfectly acceptable to them. Coprophagia usually refers to the dog eating his own feces, but it also refers to the consumption of other animals' feces. Strange as it may be, coprophagic dogs often prefer cat or horse stool over that of another dog. Deer droppings are also a choice delicacy to some dogs. The stool consistency—coprophagic dogs tend to prefer harder stools—and the presence of undigested nutrients seem to make a difference.

Why does a dog eat feces? He may be seeking certain nutrients missing in his diet, or he could be just plain hungry. Excrement that smells bad to us is pleasing to dogs. They also might be obeying a primitive instinct that tells them to get rid of the evidence that might betray them to predators.

Coprophagia will usually bring on diarrhea, which may be all the influence your dog needs to kick the habit. If not, there are steps you can take to deter the behavior.

Solution

A coprophagic dog owner should first determine if the dog's diet is nutritionally complete. Veterinarians have found that diets low in fiber and high in starch may increase the urge to eat feces, so adding fiber to your dog's food is worth a try. Mix a teaspoon of unprocessed bran into his food, and your Staffy will never know the difference at mealtime.

If the vet finds no medical reason behind the coprophagic behavior, modify your dog's environment as a means of control. Clean up animal waste from your yard, and distract your dog if you catch him nibbling on nasty stuff. Verbal reprimands won't work when delectable droppings are at stake. You can also purchase commercial products that you sprinkle on your dog's food to render his feces unappetizing without compromising the good taste of his food. Fortunately, coprophagia is most often seen in young puppies who usually grow out of the habit by their first birthday.

Digging

Humans may consider digging a destructive behavior, but to a Staffy, it's not only just plain fun—it comes naturally. Staffies are terriers, whose job historically has been to ferret (pardon the pun) out vermin. We also tend to forget that, in domesticating dogs, we have relieved them of the daily burden of finding food, water, and shelter. Without any activity to replace this task, unchanneled energy may result in holes in the yard and garden. Digging may indicate boredom, not to mention the adventure of exploring those endlessly tempting smells in dirt.

Solution

Digging is one of the most challenging behaviors to correct

because it's difficult to catch the dog in the act. Dog owners are usually away from home or busy inside the house while the digging takes place. By the time they notice the holes, the damage is done and it's too late to chastise. A dog won't connect your reprimand with something he did hours earlier.

In addition to the landscaping havoc that digging can wreak, you must make sure that your Staffy doesn't dig his way out of your fenced yard or kennel area. It's not unheard of for a determined Staffy to dig an escape route underneath a fence if he smells a dog in heat or some other enticement. The first step in dealing with a digging Staffy is to reinforce the fence below ground so that escape by tunneling is impossible. This usually means laying in some kind of barrier fencing beneath the fence posts. An experienced carpenter or fence builder can help you with this.

Your next concern is to eliminate boredom and mischief by ensuring that your Staffy gets plenty of play and exercise outdoors. A contentedly tired dog won't start digging just because there's nothing else to do.

Alternatively, you can solve the digging problem not by curtailing the behavior but by relocating it. Fence off a section of your yard, about 6 by 20 feet (2 by 6 m), and designate it as your Staffy's special digging spot. When you're able to closely supervise, he can have free rein of the whole yard. If he starts to dig in the "forbidden zone," use your voice to interrupt him,

To dogs, digging is an instinctive behavior.

To keep your Staffy from jumping up on people, tell him to sit when visitors arrive

and redirect him to his digging area.

Eventually, he'll prefer to dig where he's not interrupted.

As with many disciplinary issues, your commitment to correcting the behavior may be temporarily more troublesome than the behavior itself. Remember, no pain, no gain!

Food Stealing

No matter how tasty your dog's food is, your food will tempt him more. Just when you think you've put that steak far back enough on the countertop, your Staffy will prove once again that he is not to be underestimated. The problem with intelligent dogs is that they discover how to outsmart us!

Solution

If you're losing too many packages of hotdogs, it's time to make the payoff less rewarding. Place a shaker can (an empty soda can partially filled with pebbles or coins) on the counter with the food temptation. Position the can so that it will fall when your Staffy pulls down the booty. The startling noise will unnerve him, and he'll come to associate it with whatever he's stealing.

You can also utilize inexpensive training tools that operate as motion-sensor devices. Place one on the counter or table where the food item sits. When your dog gets too close or touches the device itself, it will emit a loud noise. These devices also come in handy when you want to keep your Staffy from snoozing on the forbidden sofa.

Jumping on People

Staffies adore people, so it's hard to envision one who doesn't greet visitors with more than the usual share of enthusiasm. Few people mind a cute puppy jumping against their shins, clamoring for attention. A full-grown, stocky Staffy is another matter. Even the most devoted dog lover may not appreciate a 35-pound (16-kg) Staffy charging at her white linen slacks and silk blouse.

Solution

The idea here is to teach your Staffy pup to sit quietly when visitors arrive until he is called forth to be greeted and petted. Whenever you enter your home, ignore your puppy until you have a leash and collar in hand. It won't be easy to resist the adorable bundle who's so happy to see you, but don't give in to the impulse to scoop him into your arms and let him lavish your face with kisses. Instead, slip on the collar and give the sit command. If he jumps up, tell him "No!" firmly and give the sit command again. Avoid using the term "Down!" because you want him to learn that word to mean that he should lie down. When he obeys, praise him. He'll eventually understand that anything good happens only after he assumes the sit position.

Reinforce this message by requiring him to sit before he can eat his meals, before you pet him, before you attach his leash for a walk, and before doing anything else he enjoys. This is essentially the same thing as teaching a child to say "please." Your Staffy will know that

When Puppy Misbehaves: What Not to Do

If you're not yet convinced that corporal punishment is an unacceptable means of training, consider what can happen if you hit your dog:

- He could become afraid of you and cower whenever a hand (even someone else's) comes toward his face.
- He will fear you to the point of keeping away from you at all costs.
- He will attempt to defend himself by biting.
- He could interpret a light smack as an invitation to play and become even more excited and apt to nip.

You really do catch more flies with honey than with vinegar.

if he sits for a guest, praise and attention will follow. Ask your visitors to help by not petting the dog until he sits, lest he inadvertently be "rewarded" without doing anything to earn it. When you're out in public with your Staffy, he will no doubt attract a lot of attention, and people may ask to pet him. Make him sit before allowing anyone to pet him, explaining that you're teaching him good manners. Not only will you be reinforcing the lesson of not jumping up, you'll be demonstrating what a friendly, well-behaved dog he is.

Mounting

Contrary to popular belief, mounting is not always a sexual behavior—it's sometimes a means of establishing dominance. Males and females alike are known to mount, and altering doesn't necessarily eliminate the behavior. While dogs most often demonstrate mounting behavior to humans and other dogs, occasionally they will mount pillows or stuffed toys.

Sometimes, mounting behavior is nothing more than the result of a (nonsexually) stimulated or hyperactive dog. In these situations, the behavior is called "social overture during play." It happens more frequently with adolescent, small dogs, and often stops on its own once the dog reaches maturity.

Mounting may also indicate your Staffy's insecurity with his position in the pack, whether it's with your family or with other pets in the home. He may attempt to reinforce his status by mounting. If the "mountee" submits to it, he is acknowledging his subordinate role.

Solution

The best way to avoid dominance issues is to provide solid leadership from puppyhood on. If mounting behavior becomes a problem, distraction is the best method for curtailing this behavior. If your Staffy assumes a mounting posture, say "No!" sharply and remove him gently from the posture. Give him something else to do, like perform a quick obedience command that you can reward with a toy or treat, that will take precedence over the urge to mount. Make sure that you don't give him the distracting toy or treat too soon, though, lest he misconstrue it as a reward for mounting behavior.

If your Staffy attempts to get back in the saddle again,

How to Find a Behavior Specialist

If aggression or separation anxiety persists, and no underlying medical reason is the cause, don't despair. There are professionals who can help. Your best bet is a veterinary behaviorist particularly experienced with bully breeds or a trainer experienced with problem dogs. Request referrals from organizations like the American Animal Hospital Association (AAHA) or the Staffordshire Bull Terrier Club of America , Inc. (SBTCA). Ask other dog owners, especially bully breed owners or breeders. Conduct an Internet search, or contact a veterinary school. Someone somewhere along the line will be able to direct you toward the right professional.

remove him from the posture and take him aside for a soothing talking-to. If all else fails, remove the mounting dog from the situation by crating him. Put a toy or treat inside so that he doesn't think you are punishing him. If his mounting behavior continues or escalates well into adulthood, ask your veterinarian for advice. There may be a hormonal issue.

Sometimes, mounting is nothing more than a form of play, but if your Staffy's playmate takes exception to it, there can be trouble. Intervene at the first inkling of dissension. You may want to restrict his playmates to those dogs who display similar play behavior.

Nipping

Puppies live up to the name "little nipper" for a good reason. When they play with one another, they mostly mouth and play-bite or nip. This is normal, instinctive behavior that actually helps teach them about the boundaries of rough play. A puppy who pesters his mother with too much nipping will get a reprimand. An emerging dominant puppy may nip a subordinate littermate who gets too frisky. The nipping and play-biting is rarely aggression oriented, but it can be a difficult habit to break. Those needle-sharp puppy teeth can accidentally skewer your flesh!

Solution

The way to correct nipping is to encourage acceptable behavior and discourage the unacceptable. If an energetic Staffy pup goes for your hand, replace it with a chew toy. If nipping the hand that pets him becomes a chronic problem, offer an acceptable chew toy with one hand while scratching him behind the ears with the other. The puppy will learn to associate chewing on the toy with the pleasure of being petted. You're essentially redirecting the puppy's enthusiasm for play in a way that's acceptable for humans.

To discourage nipping, teach the puppy that the action results in the withdrawal of love and attention. When he nips you, look at him directly and say "Ouch!" Some people make a puppy-like yip, as this is what a puppy hears if he's too rough on his littermates. Ignore the puppy until he's calm, even if it means leaving the room. When he's calm again, try the chew

Did I Do That?

The "guilty" look dogs often wear when you're chastising them for some misdeed is actually a submissive posture that says "I know you're angry with me, but I don't know why, so I'm frightened." If you discover mischief after the fact, count to ten, eat some chocolate, or do whatever you need to do to keep yourself from getting angry at your Staffy. He won't understand why you're angry and may only repeat the behavior.

toy-while-petting method again. In all likelihood, your Staffy will outgrow the nipping stage and move on to the more gratifying adolescent play of tugging and wrestling.

Separation Anxiety

A Staffy who cries, howls, or barks incessantly when you leave the house is telling you he doesn't like being left alone. Separation anxiety can also be manifested in destructive behavior like chewing furniture or urinating on your bed or clothes. Social animals like dogs prefer not to be left alone, and it's hard to establish that fine line between "mother love" of your needy new puppy and "smother love," which can foster a puppy's extreme dependence on your company.

Separation anxiety is another good reason to successfully crate train your Staffy. He must learn that he is in a safe, comfortable place while you're out for a while, where he can't do damage to himself or your belongings.

Solution

The most important thing to remember when dealing with

A qualified behaviorist may be able to help you resolve your dog's problem behavior.

separation anxiety is to trivialize your comings and goings. Don't drag out your departure with a sad farewell, and don't return to hug and kiss your Staffy as though you've been away for weeks. When it's time to leave, casually give him a treat or a peanut butter-stuffed toy in his crate, close the door, and leave. If you wish, you can turn on some soothing radio music to keep him company while you're out. When you return home, don't rush to the crate. Nonchalantly open the crate door to greet your dog, and take him outside to eliminate.

You can accustom your Staffy to staying at home by himself by leaving him for short periods, starting with five-minute increments. Put him in his crate and take a walk around the block. Gradually build up the length of your absences to 30-minute increments. He'll become used to the separations and feel confident about your return.

If you're concerned about your anxious Staffy's behavior while you're out, set up a video camera to record him. This is especially helpful if the adult Staffy is left uncrated. Place the camera out of his reach in a location where he'll likely pass the time. This will show you exactly how he behaves in your absence. If he's crated, as he should be, but cries and barks when you leave, the video will give you an idea of how long it takes him to calm down. It may relieve your own anxiety to see that he doesn't vocalize very long after your departure.

A dog with separation anxiety doesn't like being left alone.

The time it takes to show improvement will vary from dog to dog, but if separation anxiety persists in your Staffy after a couple months of diligent conditioning, consult your veterinarian. She may prescribe sedatives or refer you to a behavioral specialist.

Remember, there is a difference between separation anxiety and just plain loneliness. The latter can occur if you simply don't have the time or lifestyle to provide the companionship all dogs crave. Be very sure, before you bring puppy home, that you are ready to devote your time and love to this little guy.

Training your Staffy is the best way to stimulate his intelligence and make him a happy, pleasant dog to be around. Whether you're promenading in the show ring or strutting around town, you can be proud that you helped make this handsome, well-mannered dog be all that he can be.

Chapter

7

ADVANCED TRAINING AND ACTIVITIES

With Your Staffordshire Bull Terrier

ogs like having a purpose in life. Dogs with "jobs" like herding, mushing, or hunting really do enjoy what comes naturally. But that doesn't mean a Collie owner must go out and buy her own flock of sheep or that a spaniel owner must start riding to hounds. Staffies are terriers, born to keep small rodents in check. If you don't like the idea of him fulfilling his destiny by digging up the yard to get at moles and voles, there are a variety of organized dog activities in which you can both become involved that will bring out the best in your Staffy.

THE CANINE GOOD CITIZEN® PROGRAM

The Canine Good Citizen (CGC) program was established by the American Kennel Club (AKC) in 1989 as a means of highlighting responsible pet ownership and the importance of teaching dogs to be well mannered. All dog breeds are eligible to participate in the CGC program, even those not officially recognized by the AKC, such as the Staffy's "cousin," the American Pit Bull Terrier.

The CGC can also be a valuable tool for evaluating a dog's potential, and many dog owners who set their sights on conformation or obedience competition test the waters with the CGC program. The exacting standards of the CGC title often herald the onset of a future working dog's formal training. The program lays a solid foundation for more advanced training in fields like rescue and law enforcement. Many therapy dog programs require that all their participants hold the CGC title.

CGC training is valuable for children as well as dogs. Many 4-H clubs around the country utilize CGC as a beginner dog-training course for children. Not only does it introduce children to the importance and gratification of dog training, but it teaches them respect for dogs as intelligent, sentient creatures.

Test Steps

The CGC test has ten sections, each involving ordinary occurrences that a typical, well-behaved, well-trained Staffy should have no trouble passing:

1. Allowing a friendly stranger to approach.
2. Sitting calmly and politely to be petted.
3. Permitting handling for grooming and physical examination.
4. Heeling on a loose lead.
5. Walking calmly through crowded areas.
6. Sitting on command; lying down on command.
7. Coming when called.
8. Greeting another obedient dog without excitement or aggression.
9. Coping with distractions and distracting environments.
10. Behaving well while in someone else's care, with the owner out of sight.

While the dog is going through these paces, owners are allowed to praise and encourage their Staffy, but enticements like toys and treats are prohibited. Also forbidden are special collars used for training, like prong collars, head halters, and electronic collars. Grounds for failure include aggressive behavior, elimination or marking of territory, and whining or any other display of nervousness.

To pass the Canine Good Citizen test, a dog must be able to lie down on command.

COMPETITIVE SPORTS AND ACTIVITIES

The Staffy's enthusiastic nature, energy, and intelligence make him a natural for competitive dog sports and activities. These activities allow Staffies to channel their tenacity and energy, keeping them mentally and physically fit. There are many sports and activities from which to choose, and the Staffy may be better suited to some than to others. You'll have fun trying to decide!

As with any sport, organized or not, get your Staffy to the vet for a thorough checkup to make sure that there are no underlying physical reasons why he shouldn't participate in your chosen

In the sport of agility, a dog must navigate a timed obstacle course.

activity. Likewise, before embarking on a demanding activity like agility, warm up your Staffy's muscles. Take him for a short walk or toss a ball around to easily get his blood flowing and his muscles loosened for the competition. Failure to do so can result in injury, and you want your Staffy to enjoy the sporting life for a long time to come.

Agility

Agility is a recently organized AKC dog sport, originating in the UK in 1977 and officially being practiced in the US since 1994. All AKC-registered breeds may participate; entrants must be 12 months of age and older. Agility is a physically demanding, interactive sport in which trials are designed to demonstrate how well the handler and dog work side by side. The dog must navigate an obstacle course consisting of jumps, tires, weave poles, pipe tunnels, and more. The handler provides verbal and hand signals to guide her dog through the course. This means that the dog must pay attention to the handler while racing his way through the course. Anyone who has watched an agility trial can vouch for the dogs' enthusiasm for the sport. They have a ball!

Prior to AKC sponsorship, agility competition was first promoted in the US by the United States Dog Agility Association (USDAA), established in 1986. Both the AKC and the USDAA offer titles to winning dogs.

Canine Freestyle

The latest innovation in dog sports is canine freestyle, in which dog and owner perform a choreographed "dance" to music. An outgrowth of traditional obedience, canine freestyle broadens the scope of dog training by adding creative elements, much the same way as equine dressage does. The sport encourages originality to increase audience appeal. Routines are performed using subtle verbal cues and body language. Costumes aren't required but are frequently used, generally by the handler, although sometimes both handler and dog are in costume. While an official, organized sport, canine freestyle fundamentally celebrates the joyous relationship between dog and owner. At the same time, it demonstrates the dynamic beauty and athletic capability of a healthy, well-trained dog having a great time with his human.

Freestyle began garnering attention around 1989 in North America and Europe, when dog owners wanted a more creative showcase for their dogs' talents than traditional obedience competition provided. The first official freestyle organization was founded in British Columbia, Canada, in 1991. Other groups in England and the US soon followed, with each region developing its own style. American groups promoted more trick-based routines with costumes for both dog and handler. English groups tended to concentrate more on the dog's execution of heelwork, with less focus on costumes and creative design.

Professional dance experience is not necessary to participate in freestyle. All you need is an obedient dog and a sense of fun. For competitive types, titles can be earned in freestyle through the World Canine Freestyle Organization (WCFO). Competitive freestyle does have rules and regulations, but it's no-holds-barred in exhibition freestyle. To help you decide if you're in it for the competition or the sheer joy of prancing around with your beautiful Staffy, contact one of the freestyle organizations for information.

Competitive sports and activities allow a Staffy to channel his tenacity and energy.

Conformation

Conformation, sometimes called "showing," is a competition in which a judge evaluates each contestant against the published breed standard. The dog who most closely conforms to that standard wins. It is the best-known of all organized dog activities and is regarded as more of a subculture than a hobby. Participants take conformation very seriously, as the 2000 mockumentary film *Best in Show* good-naturedly spoofs.

Participating in activities with your Staffy will strengthen your bond.

While a certain amount of subjectivity goes along with any judged competition, conformation is much more than selecting the dog viewed as the most attractive. Dogs must meet exacting requirements and proceed through the conformation hierarchy by competing and winning at various levels. Dogs first compete within their breed's regional club for the Best of Breed (BOB) title. The BOB-winning Staffy goes on to compete for Best in Group (BIG), where he must beat out all other dogs entered from the Terrier group. BIG titlists progress to the highest level of competition, among winning dogs of all groups, to vie for the title Best in Show (BIS).

When you're just starting out in conformation, don't expect to win right away. It's usually seasoned handlers/breeders who occupy the winners' circle. Demonstrate good sportsmanship by congratulating the winners and thanking the judges, whose opinions you solicited in the first place by entering your Staffy in competition. Be professional, but remember to have fun. A dog show is the place to learn new things, make new friends, and show off the beautiful Staffordshire Bull Terrier.

Acquiring a Show Dog

If you know in advance that you want to participate in conformation with your Staffy, your search for the right puppy will be more complicated than acquiring a good pet. You will narrow your search to "show-quality" puppies within a litter born of champion parents. Experienced breeders know early on which puppies in a litter are likely candidates for conformation and which ones are "pet quality." Pet-quality pups are dogs who may not meet precise breed standards but who are happy and healthy Staffies who will give their families a lifetime of joy. Most breeders require potential pet-quality puppy owners to agree to have the pup altered. This assures that the breed standard imperfections in the otherwise desirable Staffy are not propagated in future generations. A breeder's goal is to achieve a bloodline that is as close to the published breed standard as possible to maximize the breed's potential. This can happen only if dogs who don't quite measure up to conformation standards are not allowed to breed.

Know that purchasing a show-quality Staffy is no guarantee against health problems. A reputable breeder knows about bloodlines and health testing, but she can't see into the future. A dog who tests free of genetic conditions such as hip dysplasia and cardiomyopathy may still develop related and/or unrelated issues during his lifetime. The health guarantee a breeder provides to a buyer states only what she knows now: that the puppy she sells you is free of disease or illness.

Remember that not all dog activities are created equal. A Staffy who seems just right for the show ring may not be ideal for agility competition. You'll

What to Wear When Showing Your Staffy

Your dog isn't the only one in the show ring who must be well groomed. Your appearance counts too.

- DO dress as you would for an important job interview.
- DO wear comfortable shoes, with good traction, that complement your clothes. Save the spike heels for Saturday night and the sneakers for the gym.
- DO wear outfits that allow freedom of movement while providing discreet coverage. Pants for women are acceptable if they are part of a suit.
- DON'T wear anything with a dog club logo, name, or other personal identification.
- DON'T wear colors that clash with your dog. Avoid busy prints and patterns. If your dog is dark colored, wear something light colored in contrast to make him stand out.
- DON'T wear blue jeans. Ever.
- DON'T wear anything that will draw attention away from your Staffy. He's the real star of the show!

want to discuss with breeders exactly what your plans are for your dog so that she can help you select the Staffy who's right for you.

The Measure of a Show Staffy

Before you can hope to show your Staffy in conformation, you have to learn what the judges will be looking for. We've all watched the judges

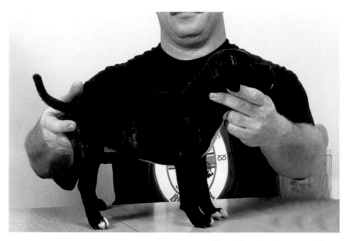

Stacking is the pose a dog strikes to allow a judge to evaluate him.

on televised dog shows who run their hands along a contestant's body or look inside the mouth. But what are they looking for? Moreover, how do the handlers learn to show the dogs' best features off to best advantage?

A show dog must master five major steps if he hopes to successfully compete in conformation. You'll need to train your Staffy to do them as early as possible:

1. **Be Sociable:** A show dog must be friendly around others, especially because the demeanor of bully breeds like the Staffy always garners such scrutiny. Can you imagine the reaction to a Staffy who acted inappropriately at such a public event as a dog show? Proper socialization is a must for show dogs.

2. **Stack Correctly:** "Stacking" is the pose a dog strikes to allow a judge to evaluate him. This regal stance shows off the Staffy's attributes and makes it easy for the judge to examine his skeletal and muscular composition. To stack correctly, a dog stands squarely on his forelegs, with his rear legs slightly stretched out behind him and the tail carried correctly. The top line should be level, with a wide front, deep brisket, or chest, and well-sprung ribs that taper to a narrower waist and hip area. First impressions are important in dog shows, so you'll want to make sure that your Staffy is an accomplished stacker.

3. **Politely Show Teeth:** Part of the overall look-see a judge performs is the condition of the dog's teeth, gums, and the set of his jaw. An incorrect bite is considered a flaw. A

Staffy's proper bite should have the outside of the lower incisors touching the inside of the upper incisors. Most dogs take exception to having their mouths handled, which can make training for this a challenge. For obvious reasons, though, you want to make certain that your Staffy is comfortable with someone (other than you) handling his mouth and entire body. Biting the judge is not going to earn him any brownie points.

4. **Stand for Evaluation:** A show Staffy must not only stack correctly, he must stand very still in this position for the judge's overall evaluation. He mustn't flinch or shy away from the judge's hands.

5. **Gait Correctly:** "Gaiting" is showing the judge the dog's movement in a trot, which is a gait that's more than a walk but not quite a run. Your Staffy's gait will be evaluated for soundness, fluidity, and the efficiency with which his separate body parts work together.
The judge will examine the dog's gait from three different vantage points: from the side, moving directly away from the judge, and coming right toward the judge. The dog must always be on the handler's left side and between the handler and the judge.

AKC Showing

The AKC offers three types of conformation shows: all-breed, which includes all dog breeds recognized by the AKC; specialty show, which is for a single breed and usually sponsored by the breed's parent club; and group show, which includes all breeds belonging to a specific group. In the case of Staffies, this would be the Terrier Group.

To receive the AKC's highest honor, the Champion of Record title, a dog must amass 15 points at shows from at least three different judges, two shows of which must be majors. A major is a three-, four-, or five-point win. The number of

If you know in advance that you'd like to participate in conformation with a Staffy, you must search for a show-quality puppy.

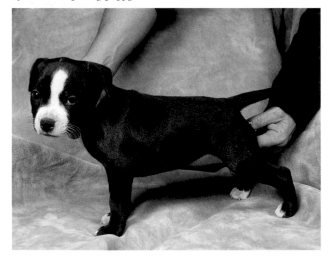

points per win is determined by the number of dogs entered in the show on that particular day. The number of points awarded varies with the breed. Winning a show for a popular breed (like Labrador Retrievers) will garner a dog fewer points than will winning a show for a less commonly seen breed (like Gordon Setters). As in most competitions, entrants must meet certain eligibility requirements. To show your Staffy in official AKC conformation, he must:

- be individually registered with the AKC
- be at least six months old
- meet any eligibility requirements listed in the written breed standards

Immediate disqualifications for the Staffy include:

- a dog who is altered (which defeats conformation's purpose of exhibiting and assessing breeding stock)
- black-and-tan or liver coloring

UK Showing

Because the Staffy's roots are in England, it's worth a look at how dog showing in the UK compares to conformation in the US. Both share the same bottom line: training for you and your Staffy is the first step on the road to conformation—or Ringcraft, as it is called in Britain—championships.

The British equivalent to the AKC, the Kennel Club (KC) is the first place to look for information on Ringcraft exhibition. The KC's publication, the *Kennel Gazette*, is a good source for learning about the show scene. Like the AKC, the KC is a "club of clubs," with about 2,000 dog clubs composing its membership. These breed clubs comprise different categories that cater to dog owners' varying interests. Popular breeds will have more clubs within the KC than will the rarer breeds. The ubiquitous Staffy has 18 breed clubs in Great Britain. Staffy owners ready to get serious about showing their dogs are wise to join their nearest Staffy club to learn the ropes from experienced members.

At a dog show, a dog is judged against the standard for the breed.

Flyball

Most athletic dogs love playing with tennis balls, and this sport is tailor-made for them. Flyball competition consists of relay teams of four dogs and their owners, competing against the other teams. One dog from each team simultaneously runs down a course with hurdles to jump, triggering a mechanism that spits out a tennis ball. The dog catches the ball and runs back through the course to the starting line. When he reaches the starting position, the next dog on the team takes his turn. The first team to finish wins the race. Flyball is organized in the US by the North American Flyball Association (NAFA), which sponsors events around the country.

Energetic Staffies can enjoy flyball as much as the next breed, but remember that some breeds are naturally faster and more agile than Staffies. Forget the pressure of real competition in flyball and just have fun!

Go-to-Ground

Dog sports are usually open to all breeds, but some breeds are naturally better suited to certain sports than others. For instance, field trialing is best performed by dogs in the Sporting and Hound Groups. Lure coursing is best for sight hounds like the Greyhound and Afghan Hound. Herding trials are perfect for dogs in the Herding Group, such as the Australian Cattle Dog and the Border Collie. Go-to-ground (GTG) has "terrier" written all over it.

GTG is an activity in which the dog navigates his way through a course scented with the alluring aroma of rodent urine. The "quarry" at the course's end is usually some kind of domestic rodent, safely caged. The dog contestant can see and smell the prey but will not be able

Tie a Yellow Ribbon

An AKC award-winning dog receives a ribbon from the judge that indicates what type of conformation award he has won:

- Blue — first place in any regular class
- Red — second place in each class
- Yellow — third place in each class
- White — fourth place in each class
- Purple — Winner's Dog and Winner's Bitch classes
- Purple and White — Runners-up in Winner's Dog and Winner's Bitch classes
- Blue and White — Best of Winner's (chosen between Winner's Dog and Winner's Bitch)
- Purple and Gold — Best in Breed in each competition
- Red and White — Best of Opposite Sex (to Best in Breed Winner)
- Red, White, and Blue — Best in Show

Staffies are well suited to go-to-ground because they have the terrier instinct to seek out burrowing vermin.

to get at it. Good canine sportsmanship doesn't include gratuitous killing of another animal.

Staffies are well suited to this sport because they are, after all, terriers. Blended in with the breed's fighting origins is the terrier instinct to seek out burrowing vermin. Dogs are never happier than when they're performing the job nature intended them to have. If they get to spend time with their humans while performing this activity, so much the better.

The GTG course is a series of three-sided tunnels constructed from 1-foot by 10-feet (0.3- by 3-m) lengths of board. The boards are buried underground and reinforced with wood braces, but the tunnel "floor" is earth. A number of right-angle turns are built into the course that correspond to the level of expertise. The dark interior and earth floor mimic a real rodent's tunnel.

The Staffy's terrier instincts have been bred thin over the decades, so he may not shine at GTG the way a Rat Terrier or Jack Russell might. The Staffy's stocky body isn't ideal for racing through narrow underground tunnels. But if GTG is what interests you, your eager-to-please Staffy will give it his all.

Obedience

You've worked hard at obedience training at home and in the classroom, and you are proud of your Staffy's accomplishments. What better place to show off his skills than in obedience competition?

Obedience competition showcases an owner/handler's training ability and the Staffy's ability to perform on command. Obedience trials in the US date back to the 1930s, when the sport's pioneer, Helen Whitehouse Walker, designed a series of exercises patterned after those of the Associated Sheep, Police, and Army Dog Society of Great Britain. Today, more than 2,000 obedience trials are held yearly in the US, with more than 100,000 dogs competing. Your Staffy doesn't have to be a conformation winner or contestant to participate, meaning that even your altered or liver-colored Staffy can partake in obedience activities.

Obedience competition is divided into three progressive levels:

- Novice: Entrants compete for the title of Champion Dog (CD).
- Open: Dogs compete for the title of Companion Dog Excellent (CDX).
- Utility: Contestants vie for the top title of Utility Dog (UD).

These levels are subdivided into Class A for show beginners, and Class B for experienced handlers. Out of a possible 200 points, a competitor must be awarded at least 170 to earn a "leg," or qualification. A dog needs three legs to earn an obedience title. Points are scored for completion of certain exercises in which possible points range from 20 to 40. The dog must score at least 50 percent of the available points in each exercise.

Dog Sports and Safety

Most of the same common-sense guidelines for human athletes apply to Staffies as well:

- Before embarking on any activity, have your vet check your Staffy to make sure that he is in the best of health and able to handle the physical challenges of your chosen sport.
- Condition (warm up) your Staffy before any event, and keep him in top condition between events.
- Keep your Staffy properly hydrated. Excited dogs often won't bother to drink at an event, so give him plenty of water the day before the event. Bring some water from home so that he won't be repelled by "unfamiliar" water and refuse to drink it.
- Avoid ice water in very hot weather to prevent cramps. Limit water intake immediately after exercise to the amount he can drink in one minute. Cool him down with easy walking before offering more water.
- Make sure that any necessary sports equipment (halters, collars) fits properly. Check for signs of irritation by collars, leads, or harnesses.

The Staffy's loveable, affectionate personality makes him a natural at therapy work.

Tracking

An extension of obedience training, the sport of tracking tests a dog's skill at following a scent. The entrant must find articles, retrieve them, and return them to the judges. The Staffy's nose and terrier instincts will guide him through this sport, although he probably won't surpass smaller terriers or scent hounds in competition.

THERAPY WORK

Therapy dogs visit hospitals and nursing homes, bringing their special curative abilities to brighten a patient's day. The Staffy's infinite capacity for love and comfort makes him a natural choice for a career as a therapy dog. Science has proven that petting and interacting with pets, particularly dogs, can have positive health benefits for humans, such as lowered blood pressure and stress reduction. It's no accident that your Staffy comes up to you for a hug or a kiss when you're feeling down. Dogs are keenly sensitive to human emotions, and their unconditional affection can be healing.

A happy by-product of a Staffy's therapy work is that it reveals the true personality of the bully breeds. A dog thought of as a "pit bull" who is allowed to interact with vulnerable hospital patients and nursing home residents must not be as

"vicious" as rumor has it. Staffies in therapy work are ambassadors for their own and related breeds.

The first step toward turning your Staffy into a therapy dog is to find out what organizations in your region provide therapy dog services. An Internet search should provide an abundance of useful websites to get you started. You can also ask your breeder, veterinarian, or local hospital or nursing home for information. Many therapy dog services require their dogs to be CGC-certified, which serves a dual purpose. CGC title holders are self-confident dogs, and nursing home or hospital staff is reassured that the dogs won't behave inappropriately in the facility and around patients.

You may also wish to ask a therapy dog service if it requires all their "therapists" to have a bath prior to each visit. While it certainly makes sense to bring the cleanest dog possible into a health care facility, the frequency of your therapy Staffy's visits is a consideration. Frequent bathing can lead to skin and coat problems. As meaningful as therapy work is for everybody involved, you don't want to create dry skin issues for your Staffy. Check with the therapy service about bathing alternatives, or limit your therapy dog's visits to once a month, the maximum frequency at which a Staffy should be bathed.

EVERYDAY GAMES AND ACTIVITIES

If organized dog sports don't fit into your lifestyle, there are still lots of ways to stay active with your Staffy. Dogs need to feel they have a purpose within the family, and your Staffy will thrive if he knows he's your special jogging buddy or camping companion. The Staffy's high energy level needs some sort of constructive outlet, and it's up to you to provide an activity that will keep him happy and sound, mentally and physically. So get out there and play!

Walking and Jogging

The simplest way to get active with your Staffy is a no-brainer: Take a walk! Walking is such an everyday part of dog ownership that it's easy to forget it can be much more than just a potty trip. Taking your healthy adult Staffy for a brisk 2-mile (3-km) walk will benefit both of you. Dogs who get into mischief at home are often bored, and the best way to prevent boredom is with activity. Walking is also a good activity to incorporate into your dog's socialization. You're bound to meet other dogs and people out on walks, providing a good opportunity for your Staffy to learn acceptable behavior during these encounters.

Walking and jogging are also good ways to keep your Staffy's toenails naturally trimmed to a serviceable length. In fact, a sign that your dog isn't getting enough exercise is if his toenails grow too long. Paved surfaces are nature's nail trimmers.

The weather will obviously impact the frequency and length of your outings. On very hot days, it's best to stay cool indoors with the air conditioning and save the walk for less oppressive temperatures. On the flip side, if you opt for a walk in cold weather, make sure that it's a brisk one. The Staffy's short fur isn't much protection against extreme cold, so make sure that he walks fast enough to stay glowing warm or wears a sweater. Remember that a dog's normal pace is faster than yours, so if you hold him to a human's pace, he won't be getting much of a workout. Keep his speed to a level appropriate to the conditions and his capabilities.

Camping

The outgoing Staffy will surely enjoy camping with his humans. It's a nice, long outdoor excursion and yet another way to spend quality time together.

Before you get carried away on visions of toasted marshmallows, though, check on a few things. Make

sure that your destination campground allows dogs, and if so, ensure that they are also permitted on hiking trails. It's unfortunate that a handful of irresponsible dog owners abuse the privileges of camping with dogs by breaking campground rules, forcing some to ban dogs completely. As with most problems associated with dogs, it's the fault of the owner but the dog takes the blame. You can help restore goodwill by following all campground rules and cleaning up after your Staffy.

Before you hit the trails, take stock of your Staffy's cumulative experience with the great outdoors. If he's a healthy dog in his prime, his paw pads should be sufficiently conditioned and his fitness level good. Don't take a sick, injured, very young, or very old dog on such a rugged outing.

Keep your Staffy on a leash at all times. And remember that camping will expose him to all kinds of parasites. Talk to your vet about flea and tick prevention and vaccinating against Lyme disease.

Dog Tricks

A Staffy's high intelligence makes him a quick study, although his independent nature can sometimes make him stubborn. But he is eager to please you, and teaching him to perform simple tricks is a good way for him to show off for you and for you to show him off to others.

Once your Staffy has mastered the five basic commands of obedience, you can progress to "graduate work." There are the old standby tricks like *shake* and *roll over*, but he can do much more. Local trainers may offer classes in "trick work," or you can devise your own at home. Remember to use positive reinforcement and consistency when teaching tricks.

TRAVEL

As dogs become more firmly entrenched as bona fide family members, it's not surprising that consideration for your Staffy's needs becomes an important part of travel planning. Many large corporations now include pet-related expenses in their relocation packages for newly hired or transferred employees. Provided you take the steps to ensure his safety and comfort, there is no reason why your healthy, able-bodied Staffy can't journey with you.

Traveling With Your Staffy

Even if you're a devout homebody, there will be times in your Staffy's life when he will need to travel, starting with his trip home with you. Whether across town or across the country, a few common-sense guidelines will make the journey uneventful.

Car Travel

Your Staffy's safety in the car is as important as any passenger's. A car restraint for dogs is probably the most important piece of safety gear you will get, and a restraint harness ensures his safety without compromising his enjoyment of the excursion. Aside from the obvious advantage of a safety restraint in the event of an accident, the harness also prevents an enthusiastic dog from suddenly jumping up or otherwise causing the driver to lose control of the vehicle.

Another option for safely restraining your Staffy in a moving vehicle is his crate. It should be securely fastened to the seat or truck bed to stabilize it while the vehicle is in motion. A properly crate-trained Staffy will feel at ease in his "room" whether at home or on the road. Wire crates afford a view of the scenery while keeping him safe.

If your new puppy's first car ride is with you en route to his new home, remember that the strange experience is compounded by separation from his mother and littermates. He may associate future car trips—especially those that end at the veterinarian—with that first scary adventure. You can show your puppy that the car is a good place with a little positive reinforcement. Lift him into the parked car and give a treat. Take him out after he finishes. Practice this daily for a week or two, and he should look forward to hearing the word "car."

Two car-travel rules should not be broken. First, don't allow your Staffy to put his

Motoring Do's and Don'ts

Very young, very old, or very sick dogs should stay home with a responsible caregiver, but your Staffy can otherwise travel by car with you, remembering these tips:

- DO use a seat harness or firmly restrained crate.
- DO schedule potty and water breaks every few hours.
- DO feed lightly before trips to prevent motion sickness.
- DO carry all identification and medical information with you.
- DON'T leave a dog in a parked car, even with windows open.
- DON'T let your Staffy stick his head out the window of a moving vehicle.
- DON'T let your Staffy ride unrestrained in an open truck bed.

head out of the window in a moving car. Debris can fly into eyes and ears and cause serious injury. It's tempting to say "just this once" because dogs love nothing more than to drink in all those tantalizing smells rushing by, but his safety overrides your indulgence.

Second, never leave a dog in a parked car, even with the windows open. A car's interior heats up like a greenhouse to dangerous temperatures even on a mild day, and open windows don't provide enough air flow to compensate. Heatstroke is a miserable way to die, so don't leave your Staffy in the car under any circumstances.

Air Travel

Air trips can be very stressful to dogs. The loud airplane noise and pressure changes are scary for infrequent flyers. Until recently, prescription sedatives had been the norm. Some experts now believe that decreased heart and respiration rates induced by sedation are riskier than the anxiety itself. If your Staffy is scheduled to fly, consult your veterinarian on the pros and cons of sedation.

When traveling with your dog, make his safety a priority.

Crated pets who are not service dogs travel in the cargo belly of commercial airplanes unless they are small enough to fit (inside their crates) underneath the passenger seat. A Staffy meets this criterion only during early puppyhood. Pets have been known to perish in transit, but thankfully, airlines now have rigid regulations for animal carriage, reducing the incidence of illness or death. Climate and season, both at origin and destination, drastically affect air travel safety. Consequently, some airlines will not carry animals as cargo during certain months or to certain destinations. If you plan to fly your Staffy, thoroughly research the airlines' policies on transport, documentation requirements, and quarantine laws, if applicable.

Foreign Travel

Dogs in military families become world travelers, as do foreign-bred dogs who travel to their new American homes. Certain concerns for the internationally traveling dog must be addressed.

Some cultures don't hold dogs in the same regard as we do in the US, and their laws and restrictions for dogs traveling internationally can vary. Quarantine laws also vary from country to country or even within a country. Hawaii is a rabies-free state, for example, so dogs flying there from the mainland are subject to quarantine that can last up to 120 days.

Planning your Staffy's overseas flight requires the same homework as a domestic flight, and more. Contact the destination country's consulate for quarantine laws and health certification requirements. Ask about all involved airlines' pet carriage policies, considering the length and routing of the itinerary. Will the dog need to change planes? How long will his crate confinement be? How will he handle the trip? Your Staffy is an important member of the family, so don't skimp on his care in the air.

Lodging

Pet-friendly accommodations are now ubiquitous, delighting families who want to travel with their dogs. It's not uncommon for hotels to charge a small refundable deposit against any damage inflicted by your dog. Sometimes the deposit is nonrefundable and pays for deodorizing and thoroughly cleaning the room for subsequent guests.

If you make spontaneous stops on a road trip, it may be tempting to just wing it and sneak your Staffy into a no-pets hotel, but resist. If housekeeping doesn't know that the room needs post-canine cleaning, future guests with allergies could suffer. Of course, neither should you leave your Staffy to snooze overnight in your car while you stay in the hotel. Aside from temperature concerns, the risk of theft is always present.

The best way to encourage pet-friendly lodgings to stay that way is to be a model guest. Leave the place cleaner than you found it, and make sure that your Staffy doesn't disturb other guests.

Traveling Without Your Staffy

Even if you wouldn't think of vacationing without your Staffy, there may be times when you simply can't take him with you. A responsible dog owner considers this situation before it happens and makes alternative dog-care arrangements.

At-Home Pet Sitting

Apace with an increasingly pet-friendly society, professional pet sitting services are becoming prevalent. Not so long ago, a child learned the value of money by walking the neighbor's dog. Now you can find bonded, insured professionals who will walk (or run!) your Staffy several times a day, feed him, and administer necessary medications. Some offer live-in services, giving you the bonus of house sitting while you're away.

Your pet sitter should be someone you know or is referred by someone you know. Have the prospective sitter pay a get-acquainted visit to you and your Staffy. Observe how she treats your dog and how the dog responds. Clearly explain your expectations, and clarify the sitter's obligations. If she will be living in your home, outline the boundaries (e.g., no parties or visitors). If sitter and Staffy take to each other, you can feel good about the companionship your dog will have while you're away and his safety in the event of a household emergency.

Doggy Day Care

Staffies require too much activity and attention to be left alone at home all day while family members work and attend school. In such cases, doggy daycare is an appealing option that prevents separation anxiety and boredom while providing socialization.

Because of the Staffy's dog-aggression potential and society's misconceptions about bully breeds, it's crucial that he is well trained before entering a multi-dog day care situation. A reputable facility will conduct a comprehensive application process, including an on-site "interview" to observe your Staffy's behavior. Some may not allow bully breeds at all. For your part, make sure that the facility and staff are clean,

What to Look for in a Pet Sitter

- Is she experienced with Staffies?
- Does she have a back-up plan in the event she cannot get to your home?
- Is she comfortable interacting with your Staffy?
- Is your Staffy comfortable interacting with the sitter?
- Is she bonded and insured?
- Is her fee comparable to other pet-sitting services?

professional, and comfortable. Ask for references. A professional service should not balk at this request.

If everything is satisfactory, your Staffy's days will be fun-filled and stimulating. You may have to drag him away when it's time to go home!

Boarding Kennels

By far the most common source of vacation pet care, a good boarding facility is a perfectly acceptable option while you're away from your Staffy. Many animal hospitals offer boarding services, providing your Staffy with a familiar environment and a staff that can handle any health problem that may arise. Some boarding kennels resemble luxurious spas, complete with private rooms and massages.

Before you leave your Staffy for the first time at any boarding facility, pay a visit and observe the condition of the facilities and the manners of the caregivers. Find out how much personal attention your Staffy can anticipate every day. Will he be interacting with other boarders? Will fresh water always be available? Will they feed the diet your Staffy is used to? These are all important issues that should be addressed before making reservations.

Conversely, there are issues that reputable kennels will take up with you. Is your Staffy up to date on all shots? Kennels usually require all boarders to be inoculated against kennel cough, a highly contagious illness that can quickly spread to epidemic proportions in a kennel. Is your Staffy trained and socialized? Does he have any special behavior or health needs? This exchange of vital information is an important step in finding the best care for your best friend.

The Staffy's natural curiosity and adventurous nature make him a great candidate for a variety of activities, from sports to exciting travel excursions. You'll find that a well-trained, well-socialized Staffy is not only a pleasure to have with you but a delightful role model in his ability to experience life to the fullest.

HEALTH
of Your Staffordshire Bull Terrier

A happy, healthy pet is every dog owner's wish, but medical problems are bound to arise from time to time. Your Staffy's good health relies on more than preventive veterinary medicine. It involves your ability to discern when something is bothering him. Your Staffy can't tell you in words if something hurts or he's feeling ill, so it's up to you to acquire a good working knowledge of canine health and fitness. This means familiarizing yourself with typical canine ailments, plus specific physical conditions to which Staffies may be predisposed. If you learn to interpret your Staffy's body language, habits, and emotions, you can work with your veterinarian as a team to provide your Staffy with the best possible health care.

THE VETERINARIAN

Dogs in general are more stoic about pain and illness than humans, and the Staffy is especially so. Unfortunately, this is one of the traits that made him so well suited to the cruel practice of dog fighting. He is less likely to demonstrate signs of medical trouble than some other breeds. When he does exhibit a problem, it's safe to assume his pain is no pretense, so finding a veterinarian you trust is one of the most important pre-ownership tasks a dog owner faces.

Finding a Great Vet

When adding a new dog to the family, one of the first things you must do is have him evaluated by a veterinarian. This means that your vet-finding mission begins before you bring home that Staffy puppy or adult.

The first logical source is the breeder or owner from whom you've acquired your dog. Unless your Staffy has been rescued from an abusive or neglectful environment, his health care regimen will have been started by his former owner. If you live in the same area, you may want to continue using the same vet who's cared for the dog since he was born. While you're not obligated to do so, there are distinct advantages to this practice. Doctor and dog already will be somewhat familiar with each other. Many new dog owners find peace of mind in using a veterinarian who's already knowledgeable about the breed in general and the new dog in particular.

It helps to find a vet who's located relatively close by, in case of emergency or repeat visits for treatments. It's also a good idea to find out if this practice provides ancillary services like boarding, tattooing, or microchipping. If a patient requires an overnight stay, is a staff member on site throughout the night? These issues may be overlooked because they're out of the ordinary, but they are important pieces of information, nonetheless.

If you choose not to use the same vet as your breeder, talk to dog-owning neighbors and friends about which vet they use. Better yet, if you know other Staffy owners in your area, ask whom they use. You also can contact the American Animal Hospital Association (AAHA) for a list of affiliated veterinarians by state. While it's tempting to use the veterinary practice located closest to you, it may not be the best choice. Perhaps their hours are inconvenient, or they have limited boarding facilities. You should feel comfortable with your choice of veterinary professional, so take your time and select carefully.

Your Staffy's First Checkup

Nursing puppies acquire protective antibodies from their mother's milk, but this natural immunity wanes after a couple of months. By the time a puppy is ready to go to his new family, at eight to ten weeks of age, he becomes susceptible to a number of illnesses. So, it is very important to take your new Staffy for a veterinary check as soon as possible, ideally within 24 hours of bringing him home. He should have received his first wormings and shots already,

Questions to Ask Yourself When Searching for a Vet

- Is she compassionate and dedicated to her field of practice?
- Is your dog comfortable with her?
- Are you comfortable with the way she handles your dog?
- Is she experienced with Staffies, or at least familiar with Staffy-specific illnesses?
- Is she open to answering all your questions?
- Is she current on the latest veterinary developments?
- Is her practice open in the evenings and on weekends?
- Are there boarding and emergency services on-site?
- Is someone present at the veterinary office 24 hours (to monitor overnight patients)?

but that doesn't give you permission to skip this first important checkup, even if you use the same vet as the breeder. It's part of your puppy's adjustment to a new life with you.

Your Staffy needs regular preventive veterinary care to feel his best.

The initial physical exam will include taking the puppy's vital signs and temperature. A normal body temperature for dogs is higher than for humans, around 101°F (38.3°C). The vet also will examine the puppy's coat to check for parasites and/or skin problems. The ears will be inspected for signs of allergy or infection. Eyes will be examined for growths, abnormal secretions, or premature cataract formation. The vet will also use a stethoscope to listen for any heart or lung abnormalities, and will palpate the abdomen for tumors or bladder stones. The inside of the mouth will be visually examined for tissue or tooth problems. Last, the vet will check the puppy's feet. A young puppy's paw pads are still tender and pink, so they need to be checked for any puncture wounds or cuts. Long toenails will be trimmed, and your vet will ask you about your plans for heartworm prevention and future vaccinations.

This may seem like a lot to saddle on a new puppy who's already a little unsettled by a change of residence, but it's in his best interest. Your little Staffy deserves the best care you can give him, and the initial checkup is the first step on a lifelong road to good health maintenance.

Annual Checkups

The initial checkup is the beginning, not the end, of the routine health care you will provide for your Staffy. Just because a dog is healthy doesn't mean that you should skip well-dog

veterinary visits. During these annual exams, your vet may detect the early warning signs of a potentially serious health issue that can affect your Staffy's future. Early detection is the best chance for correcting an acute problem or at least slowing its progression.

Your vet probably offers a running commentary on which body parts she's about to examine, but she doesn't have time to tell you what she's actually looking for. This is why it helps to understand the physical components that together form your beautiful Staffy.

Abdomen

The vet will gently palpate your Staffy's abdomen for distension or possible infection, noting if the dog exhibits signs of pain.

Back and Tail

The vet will run her hand down the dog's spine and tail to check for irregularities. The tail should be free of cuts and bruises. Ecstatic tail wagging can sometimes make a Staffy oblivious to large objects in the way, and injury is possible.

Ears

The vet will use an otoscope, a hand-held viewing instrument, to look inside your Staffy's ears. She will check for foul odor and look for ear mites, discharge, and inflammation, all of which can point to infection. The dark, moist interior of the ear is the perfect breeding ground for bacteria, so ears should be checked regularly.

Eyes

A dog's eyes usually mirror his physical and emotional state. If your Staffy's typically bright eyes become dull and lifeless, something is wrong. The vet will routinely check a dog's eyes for any debris or discharge that may indicate infection. She also will examine them for signs of cataract development.

Heart

A dog's normal heart rate ranges from 100 to 130 beats per minute. Any significant variation is cause for concern. Heart murmurs and cardiac diseases affect canines as well as people, so early detection is the best chance for a longer, more comfortable life.

Lungs

The vet will use a stethoscope to listen for abnormal breathing patterns in your Staffy. Chest congestion may indicate diseases like bordetella (kennel cough), distemper, and even heartworm.

Mouth

The vet will look inside your Staffy's mouth for lumps, cuts, scrapes, or blatant tooth problems. A healthy Staffy's mouth has deep pink, firm gums and white, clean teeth. Extremely bad breath also may indicate an oral or digestive issue.

Nose

Contrary to popular belief, a cold, wet nose does not necessarily mean that the dog is healthy, nor does a dry, warm nose indicate illness. A healthy dog's nose usually is cool and moist, but a dry, warm nose is cause for concern only if it accompanies symptoms like cracked skin around the nose, scabs

At your Staffy's annual checkup, the vet will give him an oral exam.

163

or open sores, or excessive nasal discharge. Report any marked changes in your Staffy's nose to the vet.

Paws

Paws will be examined for cuts, inflammation, or swelling. Even when a growing dog's toe pads toughen up, they should be checked for burrs or redness, especially if your Staffy licks and chews his feet frequently. Itchy toes can indicate a yeast infection, which is easily treated but highly contagious. Toenails should be cut to and maintained at a comfortable length that doesn't interfere with the dog's gait.

Skin and Coat

The skin is the body's largest organ and reveals much about a dog's health. A healthy Staffy has a sleek, shiny coat free of dandruff or uneven patches. The vet will check the coat for external parasites, swelling, abrasions, and general condition. A dull, flaky coat can herald physical issues, emotional stress, or both.

VACCINATIONS

Conscientious canine health care has long included vaccinations against deadly diseases like distemper and rabies. The latter is required by law, which is as much for your dog's protection as anyone's. If someone is bitten by a dog and the owner cannot prove that her pet's shots are current, the victim is considered at risk for the disease. A dog with early stage rabies may not display any symptoms, and the only diagnostic test is performed posthumously. In a nutshell, a Staffy without a current rabies vaccination risks being destroyed in the unlikely event that he bites someone.

Rabies aside, controversy exists over the benefits of vaccinating your dog against disease. Some people feel that introducing toxins into a dog's body through vaccines is more harmful than helpful. And some owners of "inside dogs"—dogs who are not taken outside for much more than elimination purposes—believe that vaccinations are unnecessary for their dogs, who have little contact with the outside world.

Of course, a responsible Staffy owner knows that the breed is not one to be kept indoors exclusively, so it's fair to say that Staffies benefit from vaccination. Combination shots reduce the number of separate vaccinations a dog must endure. A single injection, like DHLPP, protects against distemper, hepatitis, leptospirosis, parvovirus, and parainfluenza. Regular booster shots throughout the dog's life will keep up his immunity to these dreadful illnesses.

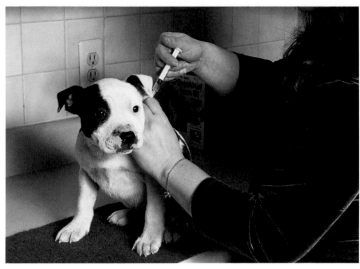

Vaccines can protect your dog against certain diseases.

Diseases Commonly Vaccinated Against

Dogs are commonly vaccinated against the following diseases.

Bordetellosis (Kennel Cough)

Once the scourge of boarding facilities, this contagious illness produces the runny nose and hacking cough of a bad cold and usually runs its course in a few days. Treatment includes isolation to prevent spreading the illness, rest in a humid environment, and (with your vet's approval) a mild children's cough remedy. Most kennels now require vaccination against bordetella for their canine boarders.

Coronavirus

Coronavirus is a multi-strained viral infection of the dog's intestinal lining that is transmitted through feces or direct contact with an affected dog. Symptoms include lethargy, decreased appetite, and sudden diarrhea that is orange-tinted, smelly, and possibly bloody. No cure is available, although fatalities are very rare and most dogs completely recover. Fluids should be administered for dehydration and antibiotics given for any secondary bacterial infections.

Symptoms of leptospirosis include fever, depression, and thirst.

Distemper

The primary killer of unvaccinated dogs, the symptoms of highly contagious distemper vary and include anorexia, coughing, diarrhea, fever, inflamed eyes, lethargy, nasal discharge, and vomiting. Early treatment increases a victim's chances for survival and may include anticonvulsants, antibiotics, eye ointment, antinauseants, and antidiarrheal medication.

Hepatitis

Infectious canine hepatitis affects the liver and is transmitted among dogs via contact with infected urine, feces, or saliva. Symptoms are similar to those of distemper, with the added symptom of intense thirst. Treatment includes antibiotics to prevent further bacterial complications, vitamin supplements, and nondairy fluids to soothe an inflamed throat.

Leptospirosis

Caused by a microorganism called a spirochete that is often carried by rats, leptospirosis causes bloody stool or urine, fever, depression, red eyes and mouth, painful mouth sores, vomiting, thirst, anorexia, and pain with movement. It is transmissible to humans, so early treatment with antibiotics is crucial.

Lyme Disease

Lyme disease is a bacterial infection spread to dogs and humans alike through the bite of an infected tick, usually the tiny deer tick. Symptoms include severe joint pain, fatigue, fever, and skin rash, which appear about two months after infection. Treatment is usually antibiotics and analgesics (pain relievers).

Parainfluenza

Parainfluenza is caused by several viruses as well as a bacterium, making it easily spread among dogs. Because the primary symptom is a hacking cough that is often contracted at boarding facilities, parainfluenza is sometimes called "kennel cough," although the term is more correctly applied to bordetella. Afflicted dogs often show no other signs of illness, and the disease runs its course, but your vet may prescribe a cough remedy and antibiotics.

Parvovirus

This deadly disease, unheard of in dogs until 1977, is readily spread through contaminated stool. Early symptoms are depression and anorexia, followed by vomiting, diarrhea, and fever. Without treatment using intravenous fluids, an antinauseant, an antidiarrheal, and antibiotics, death is likely.

Rabies

A virus-borne, highly contagious disease, rabies affects the nervous system and often presents with a change of disposition, followed by light-sensitive eyes, facial tics, stomach upset, and loss of muscle coordination. There is no effective treatment for canine rabies.

Titers

It's been common practice to have our dogs vaccinated yearly (except for rabies, which is given every two to three years) to maintain sufficient immunity against serious diseases. The controversy of overimmunization has brought to the forefront the question of how long immunization lasts. One answer is the titer test.

The term "titer" refers to the strength or concentration of a substance in a solution. A titer test is performed when a vet takes a small blood sample from the dog and has it analyzed for the concentration of the dog's immunological response to the presence of a viral disease. If the blood sample shows sufficient "memory," or levels of

vaccine titers, he is considered still protected from the disease and does not require further immunization at that time. The purpose of titering is to prevent overimmunizing the dog by vaccinating only when the need is indicated. The titer test is affordable and widely available. Ask your vet about titer testing instead of automatic booster shots.

SHOULD YOU BREED YOUR STAFFY?

The decision to breed your dog should not be whimsy. The reality of breeding is that it is costly, time consuming, and requires extensive education and research. Indiscriminate breeding only contributes to the Staffy's unfair reputation because you may be propagating genes for undesirable behavior traits. On the other hand, responsible breeding can go a long way toward producing dogs with

Responsible breeding can go a long way toward producing dogs with good-natured temperaments.

good-natured temperaments that allow the public to appreciate how wonderful Staffies and other bully breeds can be.

Breeding Pros and Cons

Contrary to some erroneous belief, breeding is not a fun, easy way to make money. You will spend a considerable amount of money on stud fees, home preparation, and veterinary assistance. The hefty sales prices of purebred puppies are not inflated by responsible breeders; they barely cover expenses. And no one has ever gotten rich on putting out their male dog to stud. Too many people breed their dogs, purebred and otherwise, without seeing the big picture, and the dogs and litters pay the price. Enough homeless, unwanted puppies exist in the world without adding to the population.

The only reason you should consider breeding your Staffy is

a true love of the breed and the desire to preserve it. Careful breeding utilizes science and thorough pedigree research to increase a litter's chances of inheriting desirable traits. Every happy, healthy Staffy pup who enters and world and goes to a loving, responsible home is evidence that bully breeds are not menaces to society. Personal contribution toward that goal can be very gratifying.

So when should you not breed your Staffy? The answer is for any reason other than for the betterment of the breed. Rationalizations, such as a female is happier when bred, or you want your children to see the miracle of birth, are unacceptable. As much as breeding takes its toll on you, it's even harder on the bitch. The entire process, from mating to whelping, is stressful and taxing. Pregnancies and deliveries are not always easy and can endanger the mother's life. Puppies often die during or shortly after whelping, for various reasons. Are you prepared to deal with that, emotionally, physically, and financially? More importantly, are you prepared to deal with the impact that breeding will have on your own life? Whelping can occur at the most inconvenient times, and delivery can take a long time. Puppies not nursing well may need bottle feeding. If complications arise that warrant an emergency cesarean section, you must be ready to deal with that immediately.

Do some serious soul searching before deciding to

If Your Staffy Becomes Lost

- Walk the neighborhood, talk to everyone, and leave your telephone number in case someone spots your dog.

- Talk to the mail carrier, paper delivery person, anyone you come across. Give them a description of the dog and your telephone number or e-mail address.

- Use a dog whistle while you search. The high-pitched sound can carry up to 1 mile (1.6 km) or more.

- Put some strong-scented clothing outside your home on the lawn or driveway. Sweaty gym socks may just be the beacon that guides your Staffy home!

- Call veterinarians' offices to see if anyone has brought in a stray dog. Also, check with all area shelters and animal control agencies.

- Post flyers everywhere you can within 1 mile (1.6 km) of where your dog was lost. Omit your name and address so that scam artists won't take advantage of it. Offer a reward, but don't specify the amount. Withhold descriptions of a few unique identifying marks or characteristics of your Staffy. You will use them for further identification if someone says they have your pet. Sadly, some people will claim they have your pet but are just looking for up-front money. Or they may try to pass off another dog as yours.

- Never search for your lost dog alone.

- If your Staffy is microchipped, notify the company with which he is registered and hope that someone will find him and have him scanned for identification.

- If he is tattooed, there is a chance that the tattoo might be seen. However, tattoos can be difficult to read, and dog thieves have been known to cut off a tattooed ear. If you do choose to tattoo your dog for identification, do it on the inner thigh.

breed your Staffy. Talk to other breeders and your veterinarian. If, after all, you decide you truly want to commit to the endeavor, you're in for an unforgettable experience.

Neutering (Castrating and Spaying)

Neutering refers to the surgical removal or alteration of certain reproductive organs in dogs. Males are castrated, a procedure in which their testicles are removed. Females are spayed. The medical term for spaying is "ovariohysterectomy," a procedure in which the ovaries and uterus are surgically removed. Females also can undergo tubal ligation, a process in which the oviducts are cut to prevent sperm from reaching any eggs.

Why Neuter Your Staffy?

The primary reason for neutering is population control. Too many unwanted pets roam the streets, struggling for survival and free to mate with other strays and produce even more homeless puppies. Allow homeless Staffies to wander free, and they are likely to be caught by animal control. And once a stray Staffy is categorized as a "pit bull," he may face euthanasia, even though he hasn't demonstrated any aggression.

If you spay your female, she will not go into heat, which means no mess for you and no marauding suitors for her. She won't be interested in escaping your home or yard in search of a mate. Because estrogen is a primary cause of canine mammary cancer, a female spayed before her first estrus will be less prone to this common malignant tumor. Spaying also eliminates the possibility of any tumors in the uterus or ovaries. On the down side, a spayed bitch may develop incontinence issues as she ages, seemingly more so than intact bitches of the same age. But medications usually help control minor incontinence, and doggy diapers are a solution for severe cases.

Neutering your male Staffy has even more obvious advantages. By removing the source of the male hormone testosterone, you may eliminate or reduce many unwanted behaviors associated with it, such as roaming and urine marking. Pheromones, the scent stimuli that alert males to females in heat, can travel great distances in the air. A neutered dog won't respond to pheromones, keeping him focused

Neutering your male Staffy may eliminate some unwanted behaviors, such as urine marking and roaming.

during training. This is why castration is preferred over a vasectomy as birth control for dogs. In addition, castration eliminates the risk of testicular and prostate tumors and reduces the risk of hernias.

When to Neuter

In the United States, most dogs are neutered between five and eight months of age, although some shelters and veterinarians will neuter males as young as six weeks. Females are usually spayed around nine months of age, before their first estrus but old enough to better tolerate the general anesthesia required for the surgery. Spaying females as young as two months may require special anesthetics and closer monitoring. Ask your breeder and veterinarian for advice on when to neuter your Staffy.

PARASITES

Parasites fall into two groups: internal parasites, which live inside your Staffy's body, and external parasites, which live on the outside of his body. Both can be the bane of your dog's existence and potentially dangerous if not treated.

Good grooming, clean living conditions, and the many types of parasite prevention treatments help protect against these pests. Talk to your vet about which parasites you need to worry about and what treatments are best for your Staffy.

Internal Parasites

Your Staffy's annual veterinary checkup will include a check for internal parasites like heartworms and intestinal worms. Responsible breeders ensure that their litters receive the necessary treatment for intestinal worms, a common affliction of puppies. Many puppies are born with roundworms, and those who aren't can become infested easily. A puppy should be worm-free by the time he goes to his new home, but that doesn't mean that you should relax worm prevention.

A dog suffering from internal parasites will show signs of general malaise, including a dry coat, dull eyes, weakness, coughing, vomiting, diarrhea, and weight loss despite a hearty appetite. Because symptoms are similar for all types of worms, you won't know exactly what kind your dog has until his stool is tested.

Heartworms

Heartworms are deadly parasites transmitted from dog to dog through mosquito bites. When a heartworm-infested mosquito bites a dog, it injects larvae into the skin. The larvae then invade the dog's circulatory system, taking up residence in the blood vessels. It can be a full six months after the bite before the worms mature. As they start to interfere with the heart's function, symptoms appear, such as chronic coughing, weight loss, and fatigue. Heart failure ultimately claims the dog's life.

Treatment of adult heartworm infestation is available, but it's expensive, lengthy, and risky, although not as dangerous as the heartworms themselves. Treatment kills the adult heartworms, but dead worms in the heart can provoke a fatal blood clot in the vessels or heart chambers. Consequently, heartworm prevention is the way to go. Your vet can tell you the appropriate age at which to start your Staffy on heartworm preventive, as well as which ones she recommends. A monthly dose of the preventive, which

A dog suffering from internal parasites will show signs of general malaise.

is usually in the form of a meaty morsel or tasty tablet, is all it takes to guard against heartworms throughout your dog's life.

There is one important caveat in heartworm prevention. The dog must be tested and found free of heartworms before starting a prevention regimen. A dog already harboring heartworms can become seriously ill from the very medication that prevents infestation. Also, heartworm prevention isn't foolproof, so a slight chance always exists that your dog can become infested. Because the symptoms do not present themselves for many months, sometimes even a year, you could innocently make your dog sick by continuing his heartworm preventive. For this reason, annual blood tests for the presence of heartworms are necessary.

Hookworms

Hookworms can cause severe iron deficiency in dogs and can be problematic for humans, too. Four different species of this bloodsucking worm are found in the United States, and the most common and most serious are found in warm climates. One species of hookworm prefers colder climates, posing a concern for dog owners in the northern United States and Canada.

Hookworms are transmitted through infected feces but cannot complete their life cycle in a human host. They will simply infest and irritate the skin. But in dogs, hookworms attach themselves to the intestines, where they feed, relocating about six times a day. Because the infested dog loses blood every time the hookworm repositions itself, anemia can develop. Symptoms of hookworm infestation include dark stools, weight loss, general weakness, pale skin coloration, and skin that is swollen and red from penetration of the larvae, usually at the feet. A number of proven medications are available to treat hookworm and prevent reinfestation.

Roundworms

Roundworms are very common in puppies and adult dogs, even those born to careful breeders. If the mother dog ever had roundworms, she may have larvae encysted in her body that can be passed on through her milk, even if an examination showed no infestation. Puppies in utero can become infested when the mother's larvae migrate to their lungs during gestation. Most likely, every puppy in the litter will be born with roundworms and require several treatments. Dogs and humans also can catch roundworms from the ground, where eggs have been deposited by other animals, including beetles, earthworms, and rodents.

Roundworms resemble strands of spaghetti and can be up to

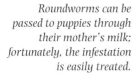

Roundworms can be passed to puppies through their mother's milk; fortunately, the infestation is easily treated.

8 inches (20.3 cm) long. Like the tapeworm, they feed off the host's digesting food. Infested puppies will eat voraciously but soon become weak from malnutrition and stop eating altogether. A pup with an acute or chronic case of roundworm will get a potbelly (noticeably larger than the typical "puppy belly") and experience diarrhea and vomiting. The condition is easily treated, but humans in the family who have contact with an infested puppy must be vigilant about their own hygiene.

Tapeworms

Tapeworm infestation comes from eating an intermediate host containing an immature form of the worm. Fleas ingest tapeworm eggs, which hatch into larvae inside the flea. If a dog ingests infected fleas, the larvae develop into adult worms that can be several feet (meters) long. Adult tapeworms feed on the host's digesting food, robbing him of nutrition. Extreme cases can be fatal.

The difficulty with tapeworm-infested dogs is that they rarely show symptoms; however, you may notice short white worm segments in the stool or in the hair around the anus. These are egg sacs that break off the adult worm, resembling wriggling grains of rice. They irritate the anus, and the dog may scoot along the floor to relieve the itching. If you see any worms in his stool, or if he scoots along the floor, the vet can treat the condition with an oral solution or an injection that dissolves the worms. Don't forget to address the issue of fleas, because they are the most common tapeworm carriers.

Whipworms

In North America, whipworms are among the most common parasitic worms in dogs. Whipworms attach themselves to the lower part of the intestine to feed. They can live for months or even years, spending their larval stage in the small intestine, the adult stage in the large intestine, and passing eggs through the dog's feces. Hosts ingest the eggs or immature worms by eating infected feces, which is why cleanup of pet waste is so important and ingestion of wild animal feces should be prevented.

Symptoms of whipworm may be only an upset stomach and slight diarrhea, which can make diagnosis difficult. The only way to diagnose whipworm is to examine a stool sample, and even this is not infallible. Dogs successfully treated for whipworm can be reinfected from exposure to the eggs deposited in the ground in feces. Whipworm eggs can survive outside in the elements for as long as five years, waiting for a host. If a stool sample confirms the presence of whipworm, the vet will prescribe a strong deworming agent to prevent anemia and kill the worms.

External Parasites

Fleas, mites, fungi (like ringworm), and ticks all think that your Staffy would be the perfect host, but guests like these will make him uncomfortable and potentially sick. External parasites can be found anywhere on the body but typically settle down on the head and neck.

External parasites are often found on the head and neck.

Parasite prevention often means introducing insecticides into your Staffy's system, the long-term effects of which concern many dog owners. No documentation suggests that long-term pesticide use poses health risks, but there is plenty of information on the dangers of parasite-borne diseases. Talk to your vet about the safest and best course of parasite prevention for your Staffy.

Fleas

Fleas are by far the most difficult external parasite to eliminate. Not only do they reproduce incredibly fast, but they actually can become resistant to insecticides. To check your Staffy for fleas, separate a patch of his fur to examine the skin. If you notice tiny black flecks that resemble ground pepper, that's flea "dirt," or excrement. If your Staffy scratches excessively, it could also be a symptom of a flea infestation. Some dogs have allergic reactions to flea bites that make them utterly miserable. Seek prompt veterinary attention to treat the skin irritation and get instructions on how to rid your home of these pests.

Mites

Ear mites are nasty critters that live inside the ear canal, irritating your Staffy's sensitive ears and producing a rusty-brown, sometimes odorous discharge. A dog with ear mites will paw or scratch at his ears or rub his head on the floor or ground to relieve the itch. If significant inflammation is present, the scratching can be as painful as it is relieving.

Two types of body mites—sarcoptic and demodex—can affect your Staffy, and a vet's examination will determine what kind is present and the best treatment. In general, she will prescribe medicine to kill the mites and their eggs and to heal the dermatological damage they caused.

- Sarcoptic mites can cause big skin problems for your Staffy by causing sarcoptic mange, making his skin itchy and crusty and raising little bumps.
- Demodex mites, which infest the hair follicles, cause follicular or demodectic mange, which may or may not cause itching. It will cause bare patches in your dog's fur and give him a moth-eaten appearance.

Ringworm

Ringworm is not really a worm but a highly contagious fungus that spreads easily among animals and humans through contact with infected skin or hair. Infective spores are constantly dropped off the hair and skin of infected dogs or people, and contact with even one spore is all it takes to catch it. Ringworm fungi feed on dead surface skin and hair cells, causing an irritating itch that develops into a scaly or raw-looking bald patch.

Ringworm is difficult to eliminate, as the fungi can be very tenacious. It can live for years in the environment and resist treatment, which usually involves a combination of topical and systemic medication. Impeccable hygiene and decontamination of the dog's environment must be practiced until the vet declares the dog ringworm-free.

Adult humans with compromised immune systems and children are most susceptible; if your Staffy is diagnosed with ringworm, and you don't have it at that time, chances are you won't catch it.

Check your dog for fleas and ticks after he's been playing outside.

Ticks

Ticks are arachnids that feed off their host's blood by burrowing their mouths into the skin. More than merely a nuisance, ticks can carry disease. The tiny deer tick is especially known to carry Lyme disease, a flu-like illness that causes fatigue, fever, loss of appetite, and swollen neck glands. Humans and dogs are susceptible to this debilitating disease. Ticks also carry Rocky Mountain spotted fever, which can cause paralysis in dogs.

Ticks come in many sizes and colors, from brown to almost blue, and are pretty easy to see on a Staffy's short coat. When removing a tick, don't do anything that may rupture or squeeze the tick's body (such as using a hot matchstick or a needle to puncture the tick) and exude any potentially infectious fluids. The simplest, safest way to remove a tick is to pull it out with a pair of blunt tweezers dedicated to the task. Grasp the tick as close to its head as possible, pull it out with a steady movement, and flush it down the toilet. If part of the tick's head remains attached to the dog's body, apply an antiseptic to the site. The head will eventually fall off.

COMMON HEALTH ISSUES

Dogs are living longer nowadays, thanks to advances in veterinary medicine and conscientious health maintenance by owners. This extended life expectancy, however, means more time for health problems to arise. The following are some common health conditions seen in many different dog breeds, not just Staffies.

Allergies

Allergies have reached epidemic proportions today, in both animals and humans. Whereas humans tend to sneeze and have watery eyes in response to allergies, dogs typically experience itchy skin and rashes that can be just as bothersome to them as our runny noses are to us.

Allergies cannot be cured, but they can be managed with patience, tenacity, and determination. Medical treatments include antihistamines and steroids, which are effective for occasional flare-ups. For ongoing allergy problems, Staffy owners should investigate other means of treatment, such as immunotherapy. Immunotherapy is designed to desensitize the dog to the allergen by building up immunity to it through injections containing small amounts of the allergen itself or extracts from it. Many dogs respond quite well to this treatment.

Allergies can be grouped into four categories: contact, flea, food, and inhalant (atopic).

Contact Allergy

Contact allergies cause reactions when the dog physically touches a substance containing the allergen. Some of the more common contact allergens are plastic, grass, and wool.

Sometimes allergy shots can combat the uncomfortable symptoms, but lifestyle changes are often necessary. These kinds of changes can be as simple as substituting a stainless steel food bowl for a plastic one or as creative as making an alternative outdoor surface for rest and relaxation, other than grass.

Tick Removal: What Not to Do

- DON'T use a sharp implement.
- DON'T crush, puncture, or squeeze the tick's body.
- DON'T apply substances to the tick like petroleum jelly, gasoline, or lidocaine. These "folk" remedies are supposed to make the tick pull out of the host, but studies show them to be ineffective.
- DON'T apply a hot match or heated nail to the tick. The theory is that the tick will be burned and pull out of the host. Even if this method works, the risk of burning your dog is too great.
- DON'T pull the tick out with a twisting or jerking action.
- DON'T handle the tick with your bare hands.

Flea Allergy

The most common type of dog allergy, flea allergy isn't an allergy to the flea itself but to a protein in its saliva, which remains in the skin after a bite. Severe reactions can cause irritations that make the dog feel miserable and bald patches that make him look just as bad. Your vet will recommend the best way to rid your home and dog of the fleas and eggs, as well as prescribe a medication to heal the skin irritations and prevent infection.

Food Allergy

Food allergies in dogs are often caused by the same foods that cause them in humans: soy, milk products, eggs, wheat, corn, and chicken. The most likely reaction is itchy, irritated skin, although vomiting and diarrhea also can occur. Food allergies are identified only by trial and error, which can take some time. Once the offending allergen is isolated, it's not difficult to customize your Staffy's diet.

Inhalant (Atopic) Allergy

Another common type of allergy, inhalant or atopic allergies result when an allergic dog breathes in an offending allergen, such as tobacco smoke, pollen, or mold spores. Even if an allergic dog stays indoors all the time, outside allergens can find their way into the house and your dog's nose. Treatment varies, depending on allergic manifestation, but elimination

The Nose Knows

Don't rely on the old standards for determining a dog's health. If you see any of the following symptoms on your dog's muzzle, pay a visit to your vet:

- **Contact sensitivity:** Allergies to plastics and dyes can manifest in a chapped or sore nose and muzzle area.
- **Nasal discharge:** Dogs typically do not experience "runny noses." Any kind of discharge is cause for a checkup.
- **Sunburn:** Yes, dogs can get sunburned, especially if they have light-colored skin and pink noses. Repeated sunburn can lead to skin cancer, just as in humans. Ask your vet about sunblock if your Staffy is at risk for sunburn.
- **Change of color:** This could be from plastic bowls, but it could also be vitiligo, a loss of skin pigment.

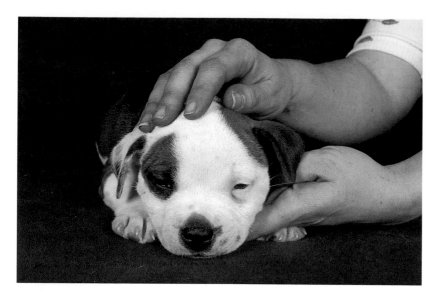

When petting or grooming your Staffy, feel for bumps, lumps, sores, or anything out of the ordinary.

of the allergen is the first step. Your vet will then discuss with you whether allergy shots, antihistamines, or topical skin treatment is in order.

Cancer

Sadly, cancer is now as prevalent in dogs as it is in humans. It rates number one out of the ten most common fatal diseases in purebred dogs. Half of all dogs who die over the age of ten die from cancer. Nearly half of all dogs who die from natural causes die of cancer.

Described as a genetic disease, the risk of cancer increases with age. One dog in five will develop cancer, the most common of which is skin cancer. Light-skinned dogs are greater targets for skin cancer, just as fair-skinned humans are. But any kind of cancer can strike any dog, any time.

These are frightening statistics, but you can't live your life in fear of a disease that may or may not show up. To do so deprives you and your dog of the joys and pleasures of everyday life. The most we can do is provide a healthy lifestyle for our canine companions and hope for the best.

Prevention

Feed your Staffy high-quality foods that meet his dietary needs, then provide the extra elements thought to ward off cancer, such as omega-3 fatty acids and cruciferous vegetables. Remember to check with your vet before adding any "human" foods to your Staffy's diet to make sure that his canine physiology can handle it. In addition, have your dog neutered, which not only contributes to population control but has the added benefit of removing the risk of cancer in the applicable reproductive organs.

Symptoms

Early detection of cancer can extend or even save your dog's life, so be observant of your Staffy. Many of the early warning signs humans are told to watch for are the same for dogs, plus a few more.

When you're petting or grooming your Staffy, feel around his body for bumps, lumps, sores, or anything out of the ordinary. Take note of his water intake (an increase or decrease in his usual drinking habits may be a symptom of illness) and how stable his appetite is. (Change in appetite is often the first sign of illness.) Monitor his energy level and mood because an ailing dog may become lethargic and depressed. If you do notice unusual symptoms in your Staffy, don't jump to the conclusion that it's cancer. Take him to the vet for an exam and diagnosis.

Treatments

Cancer treatment for dogs is much the same as for humans: usually chemotherapy and/or radiation therapy. The stage of the cancer's development is factored into the treatment plan, as well as the dog's age and overall health. Sometimes surgery can remove the cancer and/or the organ containing it, if expendable.

Cancer treatment requires dedication, as some treatments can make a dog sick. Chemotherapy reduces the body's ability to fight infection, often leading to secondary infections or conditions. The dog's body temperature may need regular monitoring at home to detect an increase in white blood cell count, which may indicate remission loss. You may have to weigh the effects of the treatment versus the quality and longevity of life without it.

Ear Disorders

In a healthy Staffy, ear care is usually unremarkable. A

routine visual check during grooming and annual vet visits are usually all it takes to make sure that ears are sound. The inside skin of the outer ear should be clean, pink, and smooth. No discharge or foul odor should be present. Your pet's behavior also will be your guide. If he paws or scratches at his ears, even if there are no visible symptoms, something may be going on deep inside the ear canal.

There is an erroneous belief that cropped ears are less prone to infection than natural ears. In some breeds with very pendulous ears, like the Basset Hound, a continually warm, moist environment may encourage ear infections. The natural Staffy ear allows plenty of air circulation. Cropping is not customary, nor is it medically necessary.

Aural Hematomas

This is a fairly common problem seen in all breeds, although most often in retrievers. An aural hematoma is a swelling of the ear flap. Blood vessels in the ear rupture, causing the space between the skin and cartilage to fill with blood or serum. The cause is unclear, although there may be simultaneous issues like ear mites, porcupine quills, or allergies that account for the excess pressure and inflammation.

Left untreated, the affected ear will become painful and scar. Medical treatments don't always work, but you should try them before resorting to surgical correction. Your vet can prescribe medications to ease the pain and make your dog more comfortable.

Ear Mites

The most common ear disorder is ear mite infestation. These parasites usually affect the outer ear canal, although other parts of the ear can be affected, too. They cause uncomfortable itching and irritation, making the dog shake his head and paw or scratch at his ears, exacerbating the irritation. You can tell if your Staffy suffers from ear mites because there will be a foul smell coupled with dark brown droppings that the mites leave in the outer ear. Treatment is usually a medicated solution to flush out the ears and kill the mite eggs.

Pet Insurance

Treatments for some illnesses, like cancer, can be costly if a dog has no health insurance. Even the many pet health insurance policies available today don't cover pre-existing conditions or certain serious illnesses. If you do plan to buy health insurance, do so when your Staffy is still young. Not only do you want the best coverage at the best price, but you'll find out if the policy restricts your choice of veterinarians. If your vet is one of the approved providers, great. If not, be prepared to choose another vet or a different insurance plan.

The proper amount of exercise will help keep your Staffy healthy and in great shape.

Yeast Infections

Yeast organisms are rarely the primary cause of ear infections, but they are quick to take advantage of prime breeding ground in ears that are already moist and red with irritation. Yeast inflammation is often a side effect of antibiotics, and it can affect toes as well as ears. Its thick, whitish discharge and yeasty odor make it easy to identify.

The worst part of a yeast infection is the intense itching it causes, and the scratching only worsens the irritation. A common home remedy is washing with a vinegar solution, but vinegar can sting, and it doesn't take care of the primary cause of the infection. Your vet will have a better treatment option for both.

STAFFY-SPECIFIC HEALTH ISSUES

Some dog breeds and breed groups are more prone to certain health conditions than other breeds or groups, but in general, the Staffordshire Bull Terrier enjoys robust health. However, keep in mind that no breed is disease-free, and any breed can develop any ailment.

The following is a sampling of disorders commonly seen in terriers, in general, and in Staffies specifically, but that does not imply that a Staffy is destined to contract any of them. It's a good idea, though, to be familiar with the conditions commonly seen in Staffies in case any of them ever confront you.

Eye Disorders

A common goal among breeders, vets, and breed clubs is to reduce inherited eye disorders. When buying a Staffy, insist on medical certification of the dog's eye history. Staffies are not prone to any specific eye disorders, but terriers as a group have a predilection to some. Responsible breeders have their Staffy parents tested by the Canine Eye Registry Foundation (CERF) to screen for any genetic eye diseases before they breed.

Cataracts

A dog's eyes have a clear lens that helps focus about a third of their vision. Any cloudiness in that lens is called a cataract. Cataracts may be minor and not interfere with vision, involve part of the lens and blur vision, or cloud the entire lens and cause loss of all functional vision.

Cataracts may develop quickly over weeks or months, or they may grow slowly over the years in one or both eyes. It is usually an inherited trait, so Staffies with cataracts should not be bred. Cataracts also can develop in diabetic dogs or orphaned puppies on a milk replacement. Some environmental factors like extreme heat, radiation, or chemical exposure can contribute to cataract formation. So can eye diseases like persistent pupillary membrane (PPM) and progressive retinal atrophy (PRA).

Cataracts or Nuclear Sclerosis?

Cataracts are not to be confused with a hardening of the lens called nuclear sclerosis, which affects geriatric dogs. This is a normal, age-related occurrence characterized by a bluish-gray haze on the lens. However, it usually doesn't affect the dog's vision, as cataracts do.

Once a cataract has developed, it is irreversible. This used to mean blindness, but now the same artificial lens replacement surgery practiced on humans is available for dogs. A small incision is made in the eye, and a hole is made in the small sac containing the lens. A special probe ultrasonically emulsifies and removes the affected lens, and the artificial replacement, called the intraocular lens (IOL), is positioned in the sac. The incision is closed with minutely small sutures, finer than a strand of hair.

Lens replacement surgery doesn't guarantee perfect vision restoration. Dogs' eyes tend to have more postsurgical inflammation than human eyes, which can cause more scarring and blur vision. But for the dog with cataracts who would otherwise be blind, the lens replacement procedure makes sense.

Lens Luxation

Primary lens luxation is a congenital eye disease that occurs when the lens moves from its normal position behind the

As a group, terriers have a predilection to some eye disorders.

cornea. Secondary lens luxation occurs when an injury dislodges the lens. The fibers holding the lens in place break, allowing the lens to shift and interfere with healthy eye functions. This disruption can lead to glaucoma or blindness, depending on where the roaming lens ultimately rests. The concern for breeders is that symptoms of this condition don't appear until the dog is about three years old, by which time the dog may have bred.

The first signs of lens luxation may result from vision changes. Your Staffy may bump into things or have trouble catching a ball, for example. Pain may cause him to paw at the eye. Treatment varies depending on the severity of the condition when diagnosed. If luxation damages the optic nerve and blindness results, no effective treatment is available. If the damaged eye is painful, it may be replaced with a prosthesis or simply removed.

Persistent Pupillary Membrane (PPM)

PPMs are vestiges of blood vessels that fed the developing eye of the fetal pup. They usually disappear by four or five months of age, but sometimes they persist and are only noticeable upon microscopic examination.

PPMs may interfere with vision, but in most cases they're of no visual significance. In extreme cases, partial or total vision loss is possible. Unless cataracts develop, no real treatment is available for this condition.

Progressive Retinal Atrophy (PRA)

This inherited disorder is a degeneration of vision cells in the retina, causing blindness. Early symptoms include loss of night vision, which can make the dog reluctant to go outside at night or into darkened rooms. Loss of day vision follows, and sometimes cataracts can occur. There is no treatment for PRA, which is why annual examinations of breeding stock by a veterinary ophthalmologist are so important. General veterinarians don't have the special equipment to check for this disorder.

Orthopedic Disorders

The best-known orthopedic disorders are seen more commonly in other breeds, but they have been known to afflict Staffies.

Hip Dysplasia

Hip dysplasia is a debilitating congenital disease that eventually can cause lameness and arthritis. A combination of genetic and environmental factors produces a malformed hip joint that causes this painful condition. In a healthy hip, the femur, or thighbone, joins the hip in the caput, or hip joint. In a dysplastic hip, the femur won't fit securely into the too-shallow hip socket. The bone can slide out of the socket, causing substantial pain.

Hip dysplasia almost always appears by the time the dog is 18 months old. Effects of the disease range from mild stiffness to severe crippling. No real cure is possible, although surgery can ease symptoms. In extreme cases, a complete hip replacement can restore mobility and prevent recurrence, but it is an

Hip dysplasia can make moving around painful for a Staffy.

expensive procedure. Prevention through genetic testing is preferable.

What can a Staffy owner do to avoid contributing to hip dysplasia? Be careful not to overfeed your puppy or adolescent Staffy. The immature bone structure of puppies may not stand up to excessive body weight, especially when the dog is young and very active. Overexercising a young dog before muscles and bones are fully developed also may contribute to future hip problems.

Patellar Luxation

Luxating patella—a kneecap that slips out of place—is a condition seen in many bully breeds. Depending on the severity of the disease, the patella may pop back into place on its own, or it must be manually manipulated back into place. A Staffy with untreated luxating patella can develop osteoarthritis in the joint, causing great discomfort. The most severe cases of luxating patella will require surgery. Here again, prevention through genetic testing is the best way to avoid this problem.

Miscellaneous Disorders

Flatulence and gastric torsion (bloat) are two additional conditions that have been known to affect Staffies.

Flatulence

It's fair to say that Staffies, like most bully breeds, have frequent flatulence. This is more of an annoyance than a health issue and always seems to make itself known at the most inopportune moments. However, most owners find the rewards of having a Staffy well worth the aromatic cost. No treatment is available for chronic flatulence, but consistently feeding a wholesome diet will keep it to a minimum.

Gastric Torsion (Bloat)

Gastric torsion, or bloat, is a serious health concern for all Staffies and other deep-chested breeds. Bloat occurs when gas, water, or both distend the stomach, causing it to swell and twist. An otherwise healthy dog can die a painful death from gastric torsion in a matter of hours.

When bloat occurs, the esophagus closes off, limiting the dog's ability to relieve the stomach distension by vomiting or belching. The bloated stomach becomes as tight as a drum and pushes against the lungs, making breathing difficult. It also pushes against the vena cava, the large vein that transports blood from the abdominal area to the heart. When this blood flow is restricted, heart failure is imminent. Only immediate surgery can save the dog's life.

Bloat more often occurs from external factors than from a genetic tendency. Studies have found that bloat can be caused by:

Bloat is a serious concern for deep-chested breeds like the Staffy.

- Strenuous exercise after a large meal and/or voluminous water intake. A stomach full of food can be twisted out of place by strenuous activity. Gulping large amounts of water can result in swallowing lots of air, which can distend the stomach.
- Gender and age. Male dogs and dogs over two years of age seem to be more frequent victims.
- Eating too fast and consequently gulping too much air.
- Eating only one meal per day. If the dog is very hungry, he may gulp his food and take in too much air. An engorged stomach can twist, starting a painful and deadly chain of events.

The symptoms of bloat are very dramatic. Seek medical help right away if you notice any of the following in your Staffy:

- dazed, "shocky" look
- excessive drooling and panting
- obvious abdominal pain and swelling
- pale, cool-to-the-touch skin in and around the mouth
- repeated attempts to vomit

Often, a dog with bloat can be saved by stomach

decompression using a stomach tube. If this doesn't work, the vet will perform emergency surgery to correct the twisted stomach, remove unhealthy tissue, and anchor the stomach in place by means of a procedure called *gastropexy*. Prevention is preferred, but sometimes gastropexy is a preventive measure performed on dogs who have a tendency toward bloat, have had repeated incidences of it, or have very close relatives who experienced it.

EMERGENCY CARE

It's an unfortunate fact of life that no ambulance is going to respond to an emergency call for your Staffy. A dog owner should arm herself with emergency first-aid information that could save a pet in need of immediate medical attention.

Purchase a canine first-aid manual and read it thoroughly. Don't wait for an emergency to happen before you read up on what to do. Keep the telephone number and driving directions of the nearest after-hours veterinary facility handy, or even better, make a practice run yourself to make sure that you understand the directions.

The following are some of the most common canine emergencies with which you should be familiar.

Bleeding

Bleeding can be internal or external. If your Staffy has suffered a major injury and there are no signs of blood, don't assume there is no bleeding. Take him to the vet

Disaster Preparedness

As we saw during Hurricane Katrina, disaster preparedness doesn't always take pets into consideration. Many evacuation shelters do not allow animals, thus posing a problem for families with pets. It goes without saying that a pet should never be left behind to fend for himself in the event of an evacuation. Before disaster strikes, have a plan in place that provides a safe haven for your Staffy. This includes a disaster kit that contains:

- four days' worth of easily stored dog food that doesn't need refrigeration
- four days' worth of water from your home or commercially bottled water
- copies of all your Staffy's documentation: vaccination certificates, licenses, registrations, prescriptions, etc.
- any medications your Staffy may require
- extra collar and leash, with identification
- first-aid kit that includes self-adhesive bandage webbing, tweezers, hydrogen peroxide, cotton balls, aspirin, antibacterial ointment, antidiarrhea medicine like Pepto-Bismol or Imodium, towel, scissors, gauze pads, latex gloves
- blanket or bedding
- waste clean-up supplies
- small toy or chew bone

Your Staffy is as important a member of the family as anyone else, so make sure that he's remembered if the unthinkable happens.

immediately.

For external and severe bleeding, use a cloth, instead of your bare hand, to apply direct pressure to the wound. A cloth will allow a clot to form. Never remove a blood-soaked pad or cloth, as it will disturb the clot and bleeding will resume. Instead, place a fresh cloth or pad on top of the saturated one and let the vet remove it once the dog arrives at the clinic or emergency

Learn about first-aid care so that you know what to do in the event of an emergency.

center. If the bleeding is from a limb that doesn't appear broken, elevate the limb with a pillow, blanket, or towel.

A tourniquet should be used only if the bleeding is very severe and other methods to stanch it have failed. A tourniquet can be dangerous in itself and can lead to loss of the limb. To learn how to apply a tourniquet, follow directions in a first-aid manual, or ask your vet to demonstrate before a real emergency arises.

Transport a dog with any kind of bleeding injury to the vet as soon as possible.

Broken Bones

If your Staffy has broken or fractured a leg, you'll know it by the telltale limp. If the injury isn't severe, your stoic Staffy may hide his pain, and you'll have to examine the joints and closely observe his walk to determine if he's broken or fractured a bone. Press very gently with your fingertips all along the leg to see if your dog is in pain. (**Warning:** You must do this very carefully—or leave it to your vet—because the pet may bite.) Lightly pinch the toes to see if he pulls away. You also may notice some swelling, hot or cold skin temperature, or a bluish cast to the skin (cyanosis). To transport your dog to the vet, pick him up

Panting is a dog's primary cooling method.

with both arms scooped underneath his body to avoid painful pressure on the limb.

If your Staffy has suffered any chest trauma, check for signs of a fractured or broken rib. His chest wall may look asymmetrical, and breathing will be painful. There may or may not be an obvious wound, and internal pain may occur when the rib is pressed. Keep him quiet and confined. Lay him on his side, with the injured rib down to avoid exerting pressure on the top lung, which will be doing the most work.

Frostbite

Sometimes occurring with hypothermia, frostbite can affect a dog's extremities: the toes, ears, scrotum, or tail tip. The skin will turn pale as the blood supply to the affected area diminishes. It turns red, swells, and becomes itchy and painful when blood circulation returns during treatment. If frostbite isn't readily treated, amputation of the affected limb and even death can ensue.

To treat frostbite, apply towels soaked in lukewarm water to the affected areas for about 15 to 20 minutes. Avoid rubbing or squeezing. If the area doesn't return to normal, seek immediate veterinary attention.

The Staffy's short coat makes him more vulnerable to cold temperatures than his Nordic counterparts. If you suspect that it's too cold for your Staffy to be outdoors for any length of time, play it safe and keep him indoors.

Heatstroke

Dogs don't sweat like humans, but they do have their own cooling system. Although they perspire a little through their paws, panting is their primary cooling method, exchanging hot air for cool. The tongue will swell to increase the surface area and allow more cooling air to pass over it. Blood vessels in the

Poisoning

Our world is filled with poisons, chemical and natural. Here is an overview of some of the common dangers lurking in our environments:

Indoors

- **Medications, dietary supplements, cosmetics:** Keep them off countertops where Staffies can get into them.
- **Household cleaners:** Keep them out of sight and out of reach.
- **Continuous toilet sanitizers:** Keep the toilet lid down at all times, or eliminate the product altogether.
- **Houseplants:** Many, such as chrysanthemums, are toxic. Find out if any of your decorative plants are dangerous, and if so, put them out of your Staffy's reach. (You can find a list of toxic plants at www.aspca.org.)
- **Foods:** Some of our favorite foods, like chocolate, raisins, grapes, onions, and macadamia nuts, are pure poison to dogs. Keep them out of your pet's reach, and share only the foods you know to be safe.

Outdoors

- **Pesticides, herbicides, insecticides:** Do not use these products on any area accessible to your Staffy.
- **Common outdoor plants:** Some can cause skin irritation, while others can kill. Take note of your landscaping and check to see if any of it poses a poisoning threat to your Staffy. (You can find a list of toxic plants at www.aspca.org.)
- **Some snakes, spiders, scorpions, and bees:** Venomous bites can sicken or kill your Staffy. Even bee stings can produce anaphylaxis, a potentially life-threatening allergic reaction.
- **Skunks:** Although not harmful physically, skunking is no laughing matter. If your Staffy has been befouled, check his eyes. If they are red and watery, he may have gotten sprayed in the face and should receive veterinary treatment. Otherwise, there are several ways to remove the oily substance in the skunk's spray that causes the odor, including commercial skunk shampoos, available at pet supply stores; a solution of baking soda, peroxide, and Dawn dishwashing liquid (keep this harsh solution away from dog's eyes); and the time-tested tomato juice method. Opinions differ as to which method is best, so consult your vet for the safest recommendation.

In the Garage

- **Antifreeze:** The sweet taste attracts pets — and kills them.
- **Paint and paint thinners:** Both are toxic.
- **Gardening or landscaping implements:** Blades can cause injury, and if tool heads have toxic residue from gardening products, can poison.
- **Car cleaning products:** These contain deadly chemicals.
- **Gasoline:** Vapors and ingested liquid can both prove fatal.

tongue then transport the cooled blood throughout the body. On sweltering days when there isn't much cool ambient air, panting can be ineffective, leaving a dog susceptible to heatstroke.

If your Staffy is exposed to very hot temperatures and you

see the following symptoms, it may be heatstroke:

- dazed expression
- increased heart/pulse rate
- moisture accumulating on feet
- rapid mouth breathing
- reddened gums
- thickened saliva
- vomiting

Immediate action will save your dog's life. For mild cases, move him to a cooler environment and give him cool water to drink. If he seems unsteady, place him in a cool bath or shower. Don't make it too cold, or peripheral blood vessels may constrict, slowing the cooling process. If you suspect heatstroke and are unsure of the severity, don't take chances. Call your vet immediately.

ALTERNATIVE THERAPIES

Over the last few decades, many pet owners have become interested in nonmedical approaches to animal health care. Alternative or holistic medicine purports that wellness and illness result from combined emotional and physical factors. Ancient disciplines like acupuncture, reiki, and herbal therapy are practiced in holistic health care, along with more mainstream treatments like chiropractic and massage therapy.

Holistic medicine advocates the use of natural remedies, usually ingredients found in plants. It has a place in modern veterinary care, although holistic vets are not always easy to find. This may change as more veterinarians include alternative methods as part of a total-care approach. It's a good idea to find a balance between conventional medicine and alternative remedies, taking advantage of all available resources to ensure the healthiest, longest life possible for your Staffy.

The following are a just a few of the many alternative approaches to canine health care.

Acupuncture

Literally translated as "needle piercing," acupuncture is the practice of inserting very fine needles into the skin to stimulate specific anatomic points in the body for healing purposes. The Chinese have practiced acupuncture for centuries, believing that good health can be restored by regulating the life force known as *qi* (pronounced *chee*). Over the past 40 years, it has become a well-known, fairly available form of treatment around the world. In the West, acupuncture is regarded as a complement to conventional medicine and is used to treat mental as well as physical conditions. Holistic veterinarians practice this painless procedure as a companion treatment for a variety of health issues, and many dog owners swear by the results.

Chiropractic

The word "chiropractic" comes from the Greek for "hand practice." The philosophy behind this treatment is the relationship of the spinal column to the nervous and circulatory systems, as well as to biomechanics and movement. Chiropractors manipulate the vertebrae to alter disease progression and relieve many joint, nerve, and muscle problems.

Herbal Therapy

Herbs have been used for their curative properties for millennia and are the most basic form of medicine available. Herbs treat a wide variety of physical, emotional, and mental ailments, as we see demonstrated today by the popularity of Saint-John's-wort for treatment of depression, black cohosh for the side effects of menopause, and the soothing scent of lavender as aromatherapy for tension.

The restorative properties of herbs are used on dogs and humans for everything from bad breath to separation anxiety. Professional herbalists know which substances have been successful in treating canine conditions, but check with your veterinarian before administering any to your Staffy. It's important to make sure that a harmless herb doesn't negate the effects of or adversely interact with any pharmaceutical treatments your dog may be taking. Also, be aware of potential allergic reactions your Staffy may experience in response to an herbal treatment. A veterinarian may have more faith in the science of pharmacology than in herbal remedies, but

Herbs treat a wide variety of physical, emotional, and mental ailments.

she has your Staffy's best interests at heart and should be open to discussion.

Homeopathy

Based on the principle that "like cures like," homeopathy formulates remedies for symptoms caused by the primary remedy ingredient. For example, syrup of ipecac is used to induce vomiting, but a homeopathic remedy for vomiting might contain ipecac. The very ingredient that causes vomiting is used to eliminate vomiting.

Homeopathic medicines are highly diluted forms of the original substance that are thought to stimulate the patient's life force to begin the healing process. As holistic veterinarians become more prevalent, veterinary homeopathy may become a helpful companion to conventional medicine.

Physical Therapy

The value of canine physical therapy was initially discovered in working with racing Greyhounds. It was important to owners and trainers that these dogs not only recover from injuries but revert to their previous performance level, or better. For the racing Greyhound owners, physical therapy was an investment against financial return; pet owners realize that physical therapy can restore their injured dog to his high-level quality of life.

Canine physical therapy accomplishes the same things as it

does for humans: It facilitates recovery and mobility. Therapies can include water exercise, ultrasound, and range-of-motion manipulation of limbs. Physical therapy increases blood flow and collagen production, minimizes muscle atrophy, eases inflammation, and gives a psychological boost to dog and owner. With the increasing prevalence of specialized veterinary practices, physical therapy is moving to the forefront of complementary medical treatment for our dogs.

Tellington Touch (T-Touch)

Named for horse trainer Linda Tellington-Jones, who initially developed the method for use in training problem horses, T-Touch integrates mind and body through movement and manipulation. Basic T-Touch consists of a series of clockwise manipulations of the soft body tissue, almost like a massage. Different from petting, it promotes a sense of well-being and relaxation that is instrumental in the healing of many physical ailments. Scientific studies have shown changes in brain wave patterns during T-Touch that support this premise, and we already know that the solace found in touching and being touched by another being has curative effects, as proven by therapy dogs.

T-Touch motion is performed by placing the fingertips on the dog's body and tracing a clockwise circle, adapting pressure, speed, and size of the circle to the individual animal. This motion can be done all over the body, including the face and even the gums (using two fingers). The ears are stroked in a sliding motion from base to tip. The experience is emotionally bonding for both dog and owner and soothing to the anxious or uncomfortable dog. T-Touch doesn't claim to be a miracle cure, nor will it change a dog's basic nature, but proponents firmly believe in its benefits. It is intended as an enhancement to veterinary medicine, not as a replacement.

THE SENIOR STAFFY

No one likes to think about it, but sooner or later your Staffy will become elderly, creating a new set of issues for you to address. A healthy Staffy could live for 12 to 15 years, but at some point he'll start sleeping more, running less, and turning gray. His hearing and vision may deteriorate. His teeth and

gums may need extra care, and his stomach may become delicate. But aging is part of life, and there's no reason why regular veterinary care and lots of TLC at home can't tackle most aging issues head-on.

Cognitive Dysfunction Syndrome (CDS)

Cognitive dysfunction syndrome (CDS) is the canine equivalent of senility in humans, the gradual deterioration of cognitive abilities. Suspect CDS if your senior dog's typical behavior changes and no physical malady is the cause. More than half of dogs over the age of eight years suffer from some form of CDS. Symptoms include:

- **Frequent elimination in the house:** Your dog doesn't communicate that he needs to go outside for a potty break.
- **Change in sleep patterns:** He sleeps more than normal during the day and sleeps less during the night.
- **Confusion:** He goes outside and just stands there, has a dazed look in his eyes, doesn't respond to your call, walks around listlessly, and doesn't recognize friends.
- **Failure to respond to social stimuli:** He doesn't tolerate petting as much, doesn't respond to you when you return home, and doesn't come to people as much, whether called or not.

Nothing is sadder than seeing your once-vital dog become a victim of CDS, but he deserves all the love, patience, and attention you can give him. No cure is available for CDS, although drugs can be prescribed to treat certain symptoms.

Diet and Exercise

The senior Staffy's metabolism slows down with age, just as ours does, meaning that he requires fewer calories from his food. Commercial dog foods usually have senior formulas that are especially created for the older dog's changing dietary needs. Some even contain supplements like glucosamine and chondroitin, which can regenerate cartilage in arthritis sufferers.

Your senior Staffy may have the spirit and mind of a puppy, but his body will tire more easily during play and need more rest afterward. Because most senior dogs develop some sort of joint difficulty, dog beds are available with special orthopedic structures or contents to make older dogs more comfortable.

Continue to provide your oldster with the love and attention he's always received, and his later years will be happy ones.

Euthanasia

Even the healthiest of Staffies will reach the end of his life with you. Modern medicine and quality care have significantly extended the life span of our pets, but this also opens them up to physical conditions previously unencountered in our dogs. It's a sad fact that relatively few pet dogs die in their sleep from old age. Chances are you will one day face the issue of euthanasia.

The hardest part of euthanasia, or the humane ending of life, is not wondering if you should put an end to your dog's suffering but when. Your vet will help you with this difficult decision, and so will your Staffy. You both have established a special communication with each other throughout his life, and that bond will serve you now. As much as he wants to please you by hanging on, the physical effort may be too difficult for him. True to form, your ailing Staffy may be in more pain than he's revealing, and you'll need to look for other signs that death is imminent. He may pant heavily, refuse food and water, or hide himself in a protected, secluded area.

Saying goodbye is never easy, but we need to love our dogs enough to let them go when the time comes. In addition to a happy, fulfilling life, there's no greater gift we can give to our pets than a peaceful departure from it.

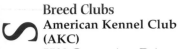

ASSOCIATIONS AND ORGANIZATIONS

Breed Clubs
American Kennel Club (AKC)
5580 Centerview Drive
Raleigh, NC 27606
Telephone: (919) 233-9767
Fax: (919) 233-3627
E-mail: info@akc.org
www.akc.org

Canadian Kennel Club (CKC)
89 Skyway Avenue, Suite 100
Etobicoke, Ontario M9W 6R4
Telephone: (416) 675-5511
Fax: (416) 675-6506
E-mail: information@ckc.ca
www.ckc.ca

Staffordshire Bull Terrier Club of America (SBTCA)
E-mail: info@sbtca.com
http://clubs.akc.org/sbtci/

The Kennel Club
1 Clarges Street
London
W1J 8AB
Telephone: 0870 606 6750
Fax: 0207 518 1058
www.the-kennel-club.org.uk

United Kennel Club (UKC)
100 E. Kilgore Road
Kalamazoo, MI 49002-5584
Telephone: (269) 343-9020
Fax: (269) 343-7037
E-mail:
pbickell@ukcdogs.com
www.ukcdogs.com

RESCUE ORGANIZATIONS AND ANIMAL WELFARE GROUPS

American Humane Association (AHA)
63 Inverness Drive East
Englewood, CO 80112
Telephone: (303) 792-9900
Fax: 792-5333
www.americanhumane.org

American Society for the Prevention of Cruelty to Animals (ASPCA)
424 E. 92nd Street
New York, NY 10128-6804
Telephone: (212) 876-7700
www.aspca.org

Royal Society for the Prevention of Cruelty to Animals (RSPCA)
Telephone: 0870 3335 999
Fax: 0870 7530 284
www.rspca.org.uk

The Humane Society of the United States (HSUS)
2100 L Street, NW
Washington DC 20037
Telephone: (202) 452-1100
www.hsus.org

Sports
Canine Freestyle Federation, Inc.
Membership Secretary:
Brandy Clymire
E-mail: CFFmemberinfo@aol.com
www.canine-freestyle.org

International Agility Link (IAL)
Global Administrator: Steve Drinkwater
E-mail: yunde@powerup.au
www.agilityclick.com/~ial

VETERINARY RESOURCES

Academy of Veterinary Homeopathy (AVH)
P.O. Box 9280
Wilmington, DE 19809
Telephone: (866) 652-1590
Fax: (866) 652-1590
E-mail: office@TheAVH.org
www.theavh.org

American Academy of Veterinary Acupuncture (AAVA)
100 Roscommon Drive, Suite 320
Middletown, CT 06457
Telephone: (860) 635-6300
Fax: (860) 635-6400
E-mail: office@aava.org
www.aava.org

American Animal Hospital Association (AAHA)
P.O. Box 150899
Denver, CO 80215-0899
Telephone: (303) 986-2800
Fax: (303) 986-1700
E-mail: info@aahanet.org
www.aahanet.org/index.cfm

American Holistic Veterinary Medical Association (AHVMA)
2218 Old Emmorton Road
Bel Air, MD 21015
Telephone: (410) 569-0795
Fax: (410) 569-2346
E-mail: office@ahvma.org
www.ahvma.org

American Veterinary Medical Association (AVMA)
1931 North Meacham Road – Suite 100
Schaumburg, IL 60173
Telephone: (847) 925-8070
Fax: (847) 925-1329
E-mail: avmainfo@avma.org
www.avma.org

British Veterinary Association (BVA)
7 Mansfield Street
London
W1G 9NQ
Telephone: 020 7636 6541
Fax: 020 7436 2970
E-mail: bvahq@bva.co.uk
www.bva.co.uk

MISCELLANEOUS

Association of Pet Dog Trainers (APDT)
150 Executive Center Drive
Box 35
Greenville, SC 29615
Telephone: (800) PET-DOGS
Fax: (864) 331-0767
E-mail:
information@apdt.com
www.apdt.com

Delta Society
875 124th Ave NE, Suite 101
Bellevue, WA 98005
Telephone: (425) 226-7357
Fax: (425) 235-1076
E-mail: info@deltasociety.org
www.deltasociety.org

Therapy Dogs International (TDI)
88 Bartley Road
Flanders, NJ 07836
Telephone: (973) 252-9800
Fax: (973) 252-7171
E-mail: tdi@gti.net
www.tdi-dog.org

PUBLICATIONS

Books
Libby, Tracy. *Staffordshire Bull Terriers*. Neptune City: T.F.H. Publications, Inc., 2007.

Rubenstein, Eliza, and Shari Kalina. *The Adoption Option: Choosing and Raising the Shelter Dog for*

You. New York: Howell Books, 1996.

Serpell, James. *The Domestic Dog: Its Evolution, Behaviour and Interactions with People*. Cambridge: Cambridge University Press, 1995.

Magazines
AKC *Family Dog*
American Kennel Club
260 Madison Avenue
New York, NY 10016
Telephone: (800) 490-5675
E-mail: familydog@akc.org
www.akc.org/pubs/family-dog

AKC *Gazette*
American Kennel Club
260 Madison Avenue
New York, NY 10016
Telephone: (800) 533-7323
E-mail: gazette@akc.org
www.akc.org/pubs/gazette

Dog & Kennel
Pet Publishing, Inc.
7-L Dundas Circle
Greensboro, NC 27407
Telephone: (336) 292-4272
Fax: (336) 292-4272
E-mail:
info@petpublishing.com
www.dogandkennel.com

Dog Fancy
Subscription Department
P.O. Box 53264
Boulder, CO 80322-3264
Telephone: (800) 365-4421
E-mail:
barkback@dogfancy.com
www.dogfancy.com

Dogs Monthly
Ascot House
High Street, Ascot,
Berkshire SL5 7JG
United Kingdom
Telephone: 0870 730 8433
Fax: 0870 730 8431
E-mail: admin@rtc-associates.freeserve.co.uk
www.corsini.co.uk/dogsmonthly

WEBSITES

www.nylabone.com

www.tfh.com

DEDICATION

In loving memory of Brooke
1997–2007

ACKNOWLEDGMENTS

Many thanks to my wonderful editor, Stephanie Fornino; to Judith Heller of Moonstruck Staffords; and to my steadfast family.

ABOUT THE AUTHOR

Cynthia P. Gallagher lives in Annapolis, Maryland, with her husband and Boxer. A member of the Dog Writers Association of America, she is the author of four single-breed dog books. Writing fiction as Cynthia Polansky, her most recent publication is paranormal chick-lit novel *Remote Control* (Echelon Press 2008). Visit her on the web at www.cynthiapgallagher.com or www.cynthiapolansky.com.

PHOTO CREDITS

DEDICATION
In loving memory of Brooke
1997–2007

ACKNOWLEDGMENTS
Many thanks to my wonderful editor, Stephanie Fornino; to Judith Heller of Moonstruck Staffords; and to my steadfast family.

ABOUT THE AUTHOR
Cynthia P. Gallagher lives in Annapolis, Maryland, with her husband and Boxer. A member of the Dog Writers Association of America, she is the author of four single-breed dog books. Writing fiction as Cynthia Polansky, her most recent publication is paranormal chick-lit novel *Remote Control* (Echelon Press 2008). Visit her on the web at www.cynthiapgallagher.com or www.cynthiapolansky.com.

PHOTO CREDITS
Photo on page 54 courtesy of H Tuller (Shutterstock).

Photo on page 70 (bowl) courtesy of Aleksandar Vozarevic (Shutterstock).

Photo on page 74 courtesy of Shutterstock.

Photo on page 78 courtesy of April Turner (Shutterstock).

Photo on page 112 courtesy of Tootles (Shutterstock).

Photo on page 158 courtesy of Phillip Alexander Russell (Shutterstock).

Photo on page 196 courtesy of rebvt (Shutterstock).

Photos on pages 5, 10, 13 (sidebar), 19, 22, 29, 30, 35, 37 (sidebar), 42, 44, 47 (bottom sidebar), 50, 53 (sidebar, top photo), 55, 58, 59, 64 (sidebar), 68, 71, 79, 81, 84 (sidebar), 88, 92, 97, 102, 103, 104, 106, 107, 108, 113, 114 (sidebar), 115, 117, 118, 119, 120, 121, 122, 128, 129, 130, 131, 132, 134, 135, 139, 140, 141, 142, 145, 146, 148, 153, 155, 156, 160, 162, 165, 166, 169, 172, 173, 179, 180, 184, 185, 190, 193, and 194 courtesy of Interpet.

All other photos courtesy of Isabelle Francais and T.F.H. archives.

Nylabone® Cares.

Millions of dogs of all ages, breeds, and sizes have enjoyed our world-famous chew bones—but we're not just bones! Nylabone®, the leader in responsible animal care for over 50 years, devotes the same care and attention to our many other award-winning, high-quality innovative products. Your dog will love them — and so will you!

Toys   Treats   Chews   Crates   Grooming